# MEMOIR

OF

# THE CONTROVERSY

RESPECTING THE

## Three Heavenly Witnesses,

1 JOHN V. 7.

INCLUDING CRITICAL NOTICES OF THE PRINCIPAL WRITERS ON BOTH SIDES OF THE DISCUSSION.

"A full and complete history of the controversy, which should enter, at large, into all its particulars, would be an invaluable acquisition to literature." — CHARLES BUTLER.

**BY CRITICUS.**

*A NEW EDITION, WITH NOTES AND AN APPENDIX,*

BY EZRA ABBOT.

BOSTON:
NOYES, HOLMES, AND COMPANY.
117 WASHINGTON STREET.
1872.

# EDITORIAL NOTE.

THE "Memoir of the Controversy respecting the Three Heavenly Witnesses" which is here reprinted consists of a series of articles which originally appeared in the Congregational Magazine for 1829, under the signature of "Criticus," and were published at London in a separate volume in 1830. The author, the Rev. William Orme, was born at Falkirk in Scotland, in 1787, and became minister of a Congregational church at Perth, in 1807. He afterwards removed to London, and became minister of a congregation at Camberwell, and Foreign Secretary to the London Missionary Society. Mr. Orme was the author of several esteemed works, as the "Memoirs of John Owen, D. D.," London, 1820; "Bibliotheca Biblica, a Select List of Books on Sacred Literature, with Notices Biographical, Critical, and Bibliographical," Edinburgh, 1824; and especially the "Life and Times of Richard Baxter, with a Critical Examination of his Writings," published at London in 1830, the year of his death. In his account of the controversy respecting 1 John v. 7, being a Trinitarian, he will not be suspected of undervaluing the arguments for its genuineness through theological prejudice; and Horne justly praises "the candid spirit and diligent research which pervade every page of his able and well-written Memoir."

The republication of the present work is due to Frederic Huidekoper, of Meadville, Pennsylvania, at whose instance I undertook its editorship. Though the controversy itself is a memorable one, and its history will always possess an interest both to the theological student and the student of human nature, it may seem to have been hardly worth while to call attention to the matter at the present day. It may be said that the question is obsolete; that the spuriousness of the disputed passage has long been conceded by all intelligent and fair-minded scholars. This is true; but a little investigation will show that great ignorance still exists on the subject among the less informed in the Christian community. The passage is still quoted as a part of genuine Scripture in volumes published by our Sunday School Societies, Tract Societies, and other religious bodies; many of the popular commentaries either give a false impression in regard to it, or pass over it in silence; and it has been used as the text for not a few sermons on the Trinity, which have been published even in the present century. Many Trinitarians, who are aware that the passage has been disputed, have a vague notion that it was at an early period fraudulently left out of some manuscripts by the Arians, and that it is now rejected by Unitarians on account of their hostility to the doctrine involved; on the other hand, some Unitarians imagine it to have been a deliberate forgery, devised for the purpose of giving support to the doctrine of the Trinity. These errors do not tend to promote Christian charity. Those who still quote the passage through ignorance should be enlightened; those who know the facts in the case, and conceal them, should be put to shame. The republication of this Memoir may perhaps contribute something to both these ends. It will also show that the interpolation did not originate in fraud, though "pious fraud" has done something to give it currency.

In the present edition of this work the extracts made by Mr. Orme from various writers have been carefully verified, as far as possible, by comparison with the originals, and many mistakes have thus been corrected; to the more important quotations in foreign languages a translation has been subjoined, for the benefit of the unlearned reader; and a few notes have been added, together with an Appendix, continuing the history of the controversy, and exhibiting the judgment of the best scholars at the present day in regard to the subject. The original text has been reprinted without omission or change, except the correction of typographical errors: the editorial additions are enclosed in brackets.

E. A.

CAMBRIDGE, MASS., *December* 20, 1865.

# PREFACE.

---

The sentence which has been placed on the title, from the *Horæ Biblicæ* of the venerable Charles Butler, is by no means intended to apply to the following pages. The author is too sensible of their imperfections to lay claim to the merit of presenting a full and complete history of the controversy of which they treat. He has neither possessed the leisure, nor the means, to enable him to accomplish so desirable a work. If, however, his efforts should induce some more favored individual; such a person as Crito Cantabrigiensis, whose acuteness and learning, calmness of temper, and powers of argument, show that he possesses every requisite qualification for such an undertaking, he will feel himself amply rewarded, though the work of the pioneer should be forgotten in the splendid triumph of the successful general.

The greater part of this Memoir of the Controversy was originally drawn up by the author as a kind of recreation from more severe labors, during hours both "few and far between," which he occasionally thus employed. What gratified himself, he imagined might afford some gratification to others. He, therefore, extended his notes, and printed them during the preceding year, in the successive numbers of a monthly publication. He has understood they created some interest in the subject; and that to a few their appearance in a separate form would be acceptable.

In that form they are now presented to the public, with some corrections and very considerable additions. Criticism he neither courts nor deprecates. He who has freely expressed his opinion of others, may expect that others will use the same freedom with him. And if this is done with candor, and with due regard to the interests of truth, though it should differ from his own, he will not complain, or be offended.

LONDON, *February*, 1830.

# CONTENTS.

## APPENDIX.

### BY THE EDITOR.

# MEMOIR

## OF THE CONTROVERSY RESPECTING

# THE THREE HEAVENLY WITNESSES,

## 1 JOHN v. 7.

THE controversy which has been agitated from the commencement of the Reformation, respecting the testimony of the heavenly witnesses, in the fifth chapter of the First Epistle of John, whether considered in a theological, a critical, or a literary point of view, is of the highest importance. It involves one of the fundamental doctrines of Christianity, embraces some of the nicest points in biblical criticism, and has brought into the field men of the most distinguished talents and learning. Happily the subject may now be examined dispassionately; as it has been admitted both by the opposers and supporters of the disputed passage, that, whichever conclusion is come to, the doctrine of the Trinity remains unaffected.

It is the object of this historical memoir to present a brief view of the progress of this interesting discussion. It is not the intention of the author to bring forward all that has been said on both sides, for that would require volumes; but to notice the principal points in the debate, the parties who have engaged in it, the subjects into which the controversy has diverged, and the state in which the matter now appears to stand.

The learned reader does not require to be informed; but for the sake of those who do, and to prevent mistakes, it is necessary to state, that the whole controversy is, whether the words in Greek and English, enclosed within brackets, in the following passage, are a genuine part of the original text.

"Ὅτι τρεῖς εἰσιν οἱ μαρτυροῦντες [ἐν τῷ οὐρανῷ, ὁ πατήρ, ὁ λόγος, καὶ τὸ ἅγιον πνεῦμα· καὶ οὗτοι οἱ τρεῖς ἕν εἰσι. Καὶ τρεῖς εἰσιν οἱ μαρτυροῦντες ἐν τῇ γῇ], τὸ πνεῦμα, καὶ τὸ ὕδωρ, καὶ τὸ αἷμα· καὶ οἱ τρεῖς εἰς τὸ ἕν εἰσιν."

"For there are three that bear record [*in heaven, the Father, the Word, and the Holy Ghost; and these three are one. And there are three that bear witness in earth*], the spirit, and the water, and the blood; and these three agree in one."

The words in dispute were omitted by Erasmus in the first and second editions of the New Testament, published by him in 1516 and 1519. This occasioned a dispute with Lee, an Englishman, who was afterwards made Archbishop of York by Henry VIII., and also with Stunica, one of the divines employed on the Complutensian Polyglot; in the course of which Erasmus promised, that if the passage were found in a single Greek manuscript, he would insert it in his next edition. An account of the controversy with Lee and Stunica will be found in Burigni's Life of Erasmus, and also in Jortin's. Stunica's attack and the defence of Erasmus will be found in the ninth volume of the Critici Sacri. The dispute with these individuals, it should be observed, was not restricted to the passage in John. Both of them attacked the editorial labors and learning of Erasmus generally, which it was their great object to vilify. That learned person was not backward to reply in his own defence.

The Complutensian edition of the New Testament was printed in 1514, though not published till 1522. In this edition the passage is inserted, whether from some Greek MS., or translated from the Latin into Greek, has been matter of dispute. At the same time, Erasmus was informed of a MS. in England, which contained the passage. This MS. has at length been found in Trinity College, Dublin, and is now commonly known by the name of the *Codex Montfortianus*. Michaelis asserts that this MS. was written after the year 1500, and is therefore of no critical authority. Mill thinks it is very modern; Wetstein ascribes it to the sixteenth century; Griesbach dates it in the fifteenth or sixteenth; and Dr. Adam Clarke, who examined it very particularly, thinks it cannot be older than the thirteenth century. In consequence of these things, Erasmus inserted in his next, and two following editions, published in 1522, 1527, and 1535, the words under dispute. While, from regard to his promise, he inserted the passage, he took care to record his reasons for doing so, and his opinion of the MS., in the following words: — "*Ex hoc igitur Codice Britannico reposuimus, quod in nostris dicebatur deesse: ne cui sit ansa calumniandi. Tametsi suspicor codicem illum ad nostros esse correctum.*"

While this sentence shows that the suspicions of Erasmus respecting the authority of this passage were never removed, it may be interesting to the English reader to know more particularly how exceedingly careful he was in forming his text of the New Testament, and that, on this very passage, he bestowed no ordinary pains. From Jortin's Life of that distinguished individual, I extract a passage, in which the views of Erasmus on the disputed passage are clearly and fully stated. In his note on the verse under discussion, he observes: —

1. "That in the Greek, only these words are found: *for there are three that bear record, the spirit, and the water, and the blood: and these three agree in one.*

2. "That this passage is so cited by Cyril in the 14th book of his *Thesaurus*, and that an orthodox father, as he was, would infallibly have cited the whole passage against the Arians, if he had found it in any copies in his time.

3. "That the same may be said of Augustin, who also cites it thus against Maximinus the Arian, although he omits nothing to establish the consubstantiality of the Father and the Son, and although he pretends that the spirit, the water, and the blood, signify the Father, the Son, and the Holy Ghost.

4. "That Beda cites the passage in the same manner as Augustin.

5. "That the controverted words are not in a manuscript of the Minor Friers of Antwerp, which he had examined.

6. "That indeed the authority of Jerom is urged on this occasion; but that this father seems to complain, in a preface which is prefixed to the Catholic Epistles, not of the Greek manuscripts, but of those who translated the Greek Testament into Latin; and that at present the words, which, as he complains, were omitted, are not to be found in the Greek manuscripts, but only in some of the Latin ones.

"'But,' says Erasmus, 'whence could Jerom discover this error of the translators? It must have been by the help of the Greek copies. But these Greek copies either were or were not conformable to our version. If they varied, as well as the Latin versions, by what indications can he show which is the best reading, and how the apostle wrote? especially since the reading which he censures was publicly used in the Church. If this were not the case, I know not what can be made of the following words: *Sed tu, virgo Christi, Eustochium, dum a me impensius Scripturæ veritatem inquiris, meam quodammodo senectutem invidorum dentibus corrodendam exponis, qui me falsarium corruptoremque sacrarum pronunciant Scripturarum.* For who would have called him a forger and a falsifier, unless he changed the common reading of the place? If Cyril amongst the Greeks did read what we now read in our Greek manuscripts, if Augustin and Beda did read so, or if they found both the one and the other reading, I see not what reason Jerom could give to prove that his way of reading was the true one. Some will say, This text furnisheth us with a strong argument against the Arians. But first, since it is certain that the manner of reading this passage hath varied amongst the Greeks and Latins, we cannot object it to them, because they will have the same right to claim that reading which favors them. But let it be supposed that the passage is incontestable, since what is said of the testimony of the water, the blood, and the spirit, that they are one (*unum sunt*, or rather that they amount to one, εἰς τὸ ἕν εἰσι), relates not to an unity of nature, but to an uniformity of testimony, could the Arians, think we, be so stupid as not to interpret in the same manner what is said of the Father, the Word, and the Spirit? especially since the orthodox explain in the same way a passage in the Gospel of St. John; since Augustin rejects not this interpretation, when he disputes with Maximinus the Arian; and since the interlineary gloss explains it thus: *Unum sunt, id est, de eadem re testantur.* This is not the way to establish the faith, but to make it suspected, by trusting to such weak surmises. Perhaps it would be better to use our pious endeavors to become one with God and with Christ, than to discuss, with an over-curious zeal, how the Son differeth from the Father, and how the Holy Ghost from the one and the other. In truth, I see not how we can prove what the Arians denied, except by satisfactory arguments. In a word, this whole passage, being obscure, can be of small service for the confutation of heretics, &c.

"'But not to dissemble anything, one single Greek manuscript hath been discovered in England, wherein what is wanting in other manuscripts is found thus: *Ὅτι τρεῖς εἰσιν οἱ μαρτυροῦντες ἐν τῷ οὐρανῷ, Πατὴρ, Λόγος, καὶ Πνεῦμα, καὶ οὗτοι οἱ τρεῖς ἕν εἰσιν. Καὶ τρεῖς εἰσιν μαρτυροῦντες ἐν τῇ γῇ, πνεῦμα, ὕδωρ, καὶ αἷμα εἰς** *τὴν μαρτυρίαν τῶν ἀνθρώπων*, &c., yet, I know not by what accident, what is in our Greek copies is not repeated here, *καὶ οἱ τρεῖς εἰς τὸ ἕν εἰσιν*, *and these three agree in one.* From this English manuscript we have supplied what is said to be deficient in our copies, that no one might take occasion to calumniate us; although I suspect that this manuscript hath been corrected and accommodated to some of our [Latin] copies. I have consulted two Latin manuscripts of very great antiquity in the library of St. Donatian at Bruges. Neither of them have the testimony of the Father, the Word, and the Spirit; and in one of them were not the words *in earth:* there was only *There are three who bear record, the Spirit, the Water, and the Blood.* In two manuscripts of Constance, after the testimony of the Water, the Blood, and the Spirit, were added these words; *as in heaven there are three, the Father, the Word, and the Spirit, and three are one.* There was neither *testimonium dant*, nor the pronoun *hi.* In a manuscript which I had from the public library of the University of Basel, there was not the testimony of the Spirit, the Water, and the Blood; Paulus Bombasius, at my request, copied out this passage from a very old manuscript in the Vatican Library, which had not the testimony of the Father, the Word, and the Spirit; and with this manuscript agrees the edition of Aldus.'

"Erasmus proceeds to show that there are Spanish editions, wherein variations are found, and that in reality nothing can be here meant besides an unity of consent. I shall add no more: this sufficeth to show how careful he was to settle the

* In this MS. it is *εἰ*.

true reading of the text of the New Testament, without paying any regard to theological prejudices, which make men seek in the Holy Scriptures only what seems proper in their opinion to establish the sentiments which they have adopted. If Erasmus lived in these days, he would see with pleasure that Jerom's pretended Preface to the Catholic Epistles, upon which so much stress was once laid, is the work of an impostor, as Father Martianai, although no extraordinary critic, hath fully proved in his edition of Jerom's version. He would see that on this particular occasion there was no reason to blame Jerom, though the judgment which he passed upon the fictitious Jerom be reasonable and just. At present this passage, and all that relates to it, hath been so fully discussed, that none except stubborn and perverse people pretend to deny that the *heavenly witnesses* are an interpolation. But there is the more reason to admire the sagacity and the judiciousness of Erasmus, who discovered the false reading." *

While this quotation shows the opinion of Erasmus, and the grounds on which that opinion was formed, it also conveys the opinion of his biographer, Dr. Jortin, on the merits of the passage. Jortin was a profound scholar, a critic of great acuteness, whose acquaintance with ecclesiastical history was more extensive and accurate than that of most men of his time. On biblical criticism he was also well qualified to pronounce an opinion, and that opinion, whatever it was, he was accustomed to express, as in the present instance, with great decision and explicitness.

Colinæus, the father-in-law of Robert Stephens, in his edition of 1534, printed at Paris, omitted the verse from want of MS. authority. It is also omitted in editions pub-

* Jortin's Life of Erasmus, Vol. II. pp. 230-233.

lished at Hagenau in 1521, and at Strasburg in 1524. R. Stephens, in his edition of 1550, inserted the passage; but marked the words ἐν τῷ οὐρανῷ as wanting in seven MSS. Beza, suspecting no mistake, and supposing that these MSS. contained the remaining words, inserted the whole passage in his editions. The Elzevir editors, following these authorities, admitted the passage into their editions, and thus it finally became a part of the received text.

In all the ancient versions it is wanting. In the Old Syriac, or Peshito, made in the second or third century; in the Philoxenian Syriac, made in the beginning of the sixth century; in the Coptic and Sahidic Versions, made between the fourth and sixth centuries;* in the Ethiopic Version, which boasts a very high antiquity; in the Arabic MSS. and most of the printed editions; and though inserted in the printed editions of the Armenian, it does not exist in the best MSS. of that translation. The same remark is applicable to the Slavonian, the oldest editions of which do not contain it. It is to be found in the printed text of the Latin Vulgate; but some of the oldest Latin MSS. want it, and in others it is interlined, or added in the margin. No satisfactory proof has been afforded that it is quoted by any of the Greek fathers; and even the adduced evidence of the Latin writers is defective or unsatisfactory.

From all the editions of the German translation of the New Testament by Luther, which were published by himself, it was excluded; a conclusive proof that the Reformer

* [These two versions, otherwise called the Memphitic and the Thebaic, are now generally supposed by scholars to have been made in the latter part of the third or the beginning of the fourth century. Münter and Woide are disposed to assign the Sahidic even to the second century; it is probably, at any rate, the earlier of the two. The Æthiopic version is usually ascribed to the fourth century. — Ed.]

wanted faith in its authority. After his death, it was inserted in his translation by some of the editors, and rejected by others, till at last its insertion became general. The modern European versions for the most part contain the passage. In the greater number of the editions of the English translation, from Tindal to the Bishops' Bible in 1568, the passage is printed either in a different character from the text, or enclosed in brackets, to intimate that it was found in the Latin Vulgate, but not in the Greek text. Calvin, Leo de Juda, Castalio, all speak of it and treat it as doubtful.

In Father Simon's Critical History of the New Testament, which was translated very incorrectly into English in 1689, the genuineness of the passage is attacked at some length.* Simon examined very diligently the King's Library at Paris, and likewise the Colbertine, containing many valuable Greek MSS.; but none of them contained the disputed passage. He found it also wanting in some of the oldest MSS. of the Latin Vulgate which he examined. His opinion is decidedly unfavorable to its genuineness; as even in regard to the Latin MSS. which contain it, he expresses his belief, that it was originally written on the margin, as a marginal note, and afterwards introduced into the text by some of the transcribers.

The following extract contains the result of Simon's investigation, and also his opinion of the manner in which the spurious words were introduced into the text, both of the Greek and Latin MSS. which contain it.

"After the most diligent search in the King's Library, and that of Colbert, in which there are a great many good manuscript volumes, I found no copy that had that passage in it, though I read seven of them in the Royal Library, six

* Part I. Chap. XVIII.; Part II. Chap. IX.

whereof are marked 1885. 2247. 2248. 2870. 2871. 2872. Some of the manuscripts have notes; but no scholiast or annotator makes mention of that passage; neither have I found it in five manuscript copies belonging to Colbert's Library, which are marked 871. 6123. 4785. 6584. 2844. Yet some of these manuscripts are only paper, and much later than the rest. There is also one in 16mo, well written, and I believe since the era of printing: yet the passage in question is not found therein, any more than in the rest of the ancient copies.

"I could produce yet other Greek manuscript copies which I have seen, whose various readings I observed; but that which most deserves our notice is, that in the margin of some of the King's and Colbert's copies there are small notes set over against the said passage, which in all likelihood have slipped afterwards into the body of the text. Take an example from the King's copy, marked 2247.; over against these words, Ὅτι τρεῖς εἰσιν οἱ μαρτυροῦντες ἐν τῇ γῇ, τὸ πνεῦμα καὶ τὸ ὕδωρ καὶ τὸ αἷμα, there is this remark, τουτέστι τὸ πνεῦμα τὸ ἅγιον, καὶ ὁ πατὴρ, καὶ αὐτὸς ἑαυτοῦ. By which we may perceive, that the author of the said remark understood *the Father, the Word, and the Holy Ghost* to be signified by the three witnesses mentioned by St. John, *the Spirit, the Water, and the Blood:* and what was formerly written by way of note, passed afterwards into the text, as it often falls out. In the same copy over against these other words, καὶ οἱ τρεῖς εἰς τὸ ἕν εἰσι, this note is added, τουτέστι μία θεότης εἷς θεός, that is, *one Deity, one God.* That manuscript is about 500 years old, and there are but very few places therein that have notes. There is the like remark in one of the manuscripts belonging to M. Colbert's Library, number 871. For beside these words that are set in the margin, εἷς θεὸς μία θεότης, *one God, one Deity;* the scholiast has also added these, μαρτυρία τοῦ θεοῦ τοῦ πατρὸς καὶ τοῦ ἁγίου πνεύματος, *the testimony of God the Father, and of the Holy Ghost.*

"This, in my opinion, is the original of the passage in question."

Speaking afterwards of the Latin Vulgate in the time of Jerome, and of Jerome's controverted preface, and endeavoring to show that the passage did not exist in that version then, nor was introduced by Jerome, he says: —

"And that which makes it further manifest, that St. Jerome was not the true author either of the preface or addition, is, that that addition is placed in the margin of most of the ancient copies, in the body of which it is not extant. It was no less than surprising, that the pretended St. Jerome should in his preface commend his new edition of the Canonical Epistles, upon the account of the change he had made, especially in the First of St. John, whilst there was nothing of such change or amendment to be seen therein. Upon which account the transcribers, or they to whom the copies did belong, thought fit to regulate the text according to the preface, by supplying, in the margin, the verse concerning *the witness of the Father, the Son, and the Holy Ghost;* which, before that time, was extant in some ecclesiastical authors. But since it was a matter of difficulty for those who placed that addition in the margin of their copies, to observe a general and perfect uniformity of words, it so fell out, that the expressions in the various copies did likewise vary. This diversity evidently proves that St. Jerome could not be the author of the addition in controversy, but that it was done by those who had a mind to adjust the text in St. John to the preface. I shall here give some examples illustrative of the manner how it was added to most of the old Latin copies of St. Jerome's Bible.

"In that copy of the Royal Library, that is marked 3584.,

in the margin over against these words, *Tres sunt qui testimonium dant,* i. e. *there are three which bear witness,* there are these other words added, *In cælo, Pater, Verbum, et Spiritus: et tres sunt qui testimonium dant in terrâ, et hi tres unum sunt,* i. e. *in heaven, the Father, the Word, and the Spirit: and there are three which bear witness on earth, and these three are one.* The writing of the addition appears to be no less ancient than that of the text. The like addition is to be seen in a copy that is in Colbert's Library, that is marked 158., where in the margin, over against these words, *Tres sunt qui testimonium dant,* these are added, *In cælo, Pater, Verbum, et Spiritus, et tres sunt qui testimonium dant in terrâ, sanguis, aqua, et caro.* And to make the text and addition agree the better, there are some of the words of the text amended or put out. There is nothing of this addition to be read in the three ancient copies of the library belonging to the Benedictines of the Abbey of St. Germans, only it is placed in the margin of one of these copies, and the addition is as old therein as the text itself.

"It is true, that it is extant in a copy written eight hundred years ago, in the time of Lotharius II. But it is strangely disfigured in that place; in that copy the reading was formerly thus, *Sunt tres qui testimonium dant,* (the words *in terrâ* being interlined,) *spiritus, aqua, et sanguis; et tres unum sunt: et tres sunt qui de cælo testificantur, pater, verbum, et spiritus, et tres unum sunt.* But some time afterwards, the words *de cælo testificantur,* i. e. *bear witness of* [or *from*] *heaven,* were defaced, to make room for these, *testimonium dicunt in cælo,* i. e. *bear witness in heaven.*

"All which different alterations are evident proofs that there was nothing of that addition in the first copies which were published of St. Jerome's Bible; for which reason it is not to be found in a certain version of the French Church, which is at least a thousand years old, and which was published by Father Mabillon, a Benedictine monk, and the first who in effect seems to have inserted that passage in his works, is Victor, Bishop of Vite, who lived a hundred years after St. Jerome."

Simon, though a Catholic, and either a sceptic or a blind devotee, was a man of eminent talents and scholarship. In all the departments of biblical literature he was profoundly versed; while he was no less distinguished for his patient and laborious researches, than for his learning and acuteness There is at the same time generally so much Jesuitism about his mode of reasoning, that it is frequently difficult to ascertain his real opinions, or the object of his aim; so that while often led to admire the scholar, we can rarely respect the man. His works in one way tend to establish the authority of Rome, and in another to sap the foundations of Revelation. On the subject of the disputed passage, however, he writes clearly and forcibly, and, I believe, simply as a critic.

Our learned countryman, Bishop Burnet, paid some attention to this subject, and in the course of his travels on the Continent examined a number of MSS., both Greek and Latin, of which he published the result. The Bishop, though a respectable scholar and theologian, was not profound as a critic. He could not account for several things in this controversy which are now easily explained. He seems to have been a believer in the authenticity of the passage himself, and was, therefore, very anxious to find it in some MS. of value. His travels are now, I believe, not very commonly to be met with, and as the passage is curious in which he speaks of this text, I will give it entire.

"I have taken some pains in my travels to examine all the

ancient manuscripts of the New Testament, concerning that doubted passage of St. John's Epistle, *There are three that bear witness in heaven, the Father, the Word, and the Spirit; and these three are one.* Bullinger doubted much of it, because he found it not in an ancient Latin manuscript at Zurich, which seems to be about 800 years old: for it is written in that hand that began to be used in Charles the Great's time. I turned the manuscript, and found the passage was not there: but this was certainly the error or omission of the copier: for before the General Epistles in that manuscript, the preface of St. Jerome is to be found, in which he says, that he was the more exact in that translation, that so he might discover the fraud of the Arians, who had struck out that passage concerning the Trinity. This preface is printed in Lyra's Bible; but how it came to be left out by Erasmus in his edition of that father's works, is that of which I can give no account: for as on the one hand, Erasmus's sincerity ought not to be too rashly censured; so on the other hand, that preface being in all the manuscripts ancient or modern of those Bibles that have the other prefaces in them, that I ever yet saw, it is not easy to imagine what made Erasmus not to publish it; and it is in the manuscript Bibles at Basil, where he printed his edition of St. Jerome's works. In the old manuscript Bible of Geneva, that seems to be above 700 years old, both the preface and the passage are extant, but with this difference from the common editions, that the common editions set the verse concerning *the Father, the Word, and the Spirit,* before that of *the Water, the Blood, and the Spirit;* which comes after it in this copy: and that I may in this place end all the readings I found of this passage in my travels, there is a manuscript in St. Mark's library, in Venice, in three languages, Greek, Latin, and Arabic, that seems not above 400 years old, in which this passage is not in the Greek, but it is in the Latin set after the other three, with a *sicut* to join it to what goes before. And in a manuscript Latin Bible in the library of St. Laurence at Florence, both St. Jerome's preface and this passage are extant; but this passage comes after the other, and is pinned to it with a *sicut*, as is that of Venice; yet *sicut* is not in the Geneva manuscript. There are two Greek manuscripts of the Epistles at Basil, that seem to be about 500 years old, in neither of which this passage is to be found: they have also an ancient Latin Bible, which is about 800 years old, in which, though St. Jerome's prologue is inserted, yet this passage is wanting. At Strasburg, I saw four very ancient manuscripts of the New Testament in Latin: three of these seemed to be about the time of Charles the Great, but the fourth seemed to be much ancienter, and may belong to the seventh century: in it neither the prologue nor the place is extant; but it is added at the foot of the page with another hand. In two of the other, the prologue is extant, but the place is not; only in one of them it is added on the margin. In the fourth, as the prologue is extant, so is the place likewise, but it comes after the verse of the other three, and is joined to it thus, *Sicut tres sunt in cœlo.*

"It seemed strange to me, and it is almost incredible, that in the Vatican Library there are no ancient Latin Bibles, where above all other places they ought to be looked for; but I saw none above 400 years old. There is, indeed, the famous Greek manuscript of great value, which the Chanoine Shelstrat, that was library-keeper, asserted to be 1,400 years old, and proved it by the great similitude of the characters with those that are upon St. Hippolite's statue, which is so evident, that if his statue was made about his time, the antiquity of this manuscript is not to be disputed. If the characters are not so fair, and have not all the marks of antiquity that appear in the King's manuscript at St. James's, yet this has been much better preserved, and is much more entire. The passage that has led me into this digression, is not to be found in the Vatican manuscript, no more than it is in the King's manuscript." *

Dr. Burnet seems not to have been aware of the reason why Erasmus did not publish, in his edition of Jerome's works, the preface before the General Epistles, or of the fact which has been clearly ascertained, that Jerome never wrote any such preface; but that it was the production of a future age. Nor is he correct in saying, that all the ancient Latin MSS. contain this preface. Father Simon clearly proves the contrary Burnet's account of the readings in the Latin MSS. which he examined, and its omission in the Greek MSS., corroborates the testimony of all others who have examined the subject.

Our learned countryman, Dr. Thomas Smith, in his Latin "Miscellanea," the first edition of which appeared in 1636, has a dissertation in support of the received reading of this text, in opposition to the views of Simon; and as Simon remarked on him, he defended himself in a second dissertation, inserted in the next edition in 1690. Smith was a very considerable scholar, who had travelled much, and was well acquainted with Greek and Oriental MSS.; but as "that which is wanting cannot be numbered," he necessarily failed in his attempt to maintain the argument which he espoused.

Kettner, a German writer, replied to Father Simon in three publications, in which he produced most of the arguments usually alleged on his side, but mixed with many absurd and trifling observations. For instance, he reckons in the second century, twenty-seven; in the third, twenty-nine;

* Dr. G. Burnet's Tracts, Vol. I. pp. 54-57, printed 1689.

and in the fourth, forty-two reasons, which might hinder the fathers from appealing to the heavenly witnesses.*

John Howe appears to have held the authenticity of the received reading, and refers with approbation to Hammond's note on the passage.† That note, though learned, will not satisfy any who are acquainted with the real merits and present state of the controversy. Mr. Oxlee gives the following very accurate account of Hammond's argument; to which he annexes an admirable answer.

"The grounds on which Dr. Hammond has erected his defence, are, first of all, That the ordinary reading hath the authority of many ancient, and all but one, printed copies; That the omission might easily have been made by an error of transcription, owing to the *Homœoteleuton;* That many copies have ἐν τῇ γῇ, *on the earth*, without the former verse; which shows, that this error of omission was the first committed; That it is not imaginable, if the manuscripts which contain it not, be correct, how the reading of the ordinary copies could have got in, except by gross fraud and forgery; That, if any fraud were used, it were much more probable that the Arians had thrust it out, than that it had been interpolated by the orthodox, who could have done very well without it; That in St. Cyprian the words are distinctly found, as also in Tertullian; That it is allowed of St. Jerome, that he asserted the truth of our reading from the Greek copies which he had; and defended it against all, publicly complaining and contesting it, that in those copies where it was wanted, it was omitted or erased by the fraud of the heretics; That St. Ambrose saith, that the heretics did erase that place.

* Porson's Letters to Travis, Pref. p. iii. Ed. 1790. Kettner's works appeared between the years 1696 and 1713.

† Howe's Works, Vol. VII. pp. 3, 4.

"Such are the arguments from which Dr. Hammond has constructed his *learned* defence; and of those eight arguments, six at least are wholly groundless, being bottomed in ignorance and mistake; whilst the remaining two are justly disputed. So far from the ordinary reading having the authority of *many* ancient copies, there is but one copy in all forthcoming, that contains it in any shape; and not even so much as one that exhibits it in its present form. Then as to the printed copies, instead of *one*, there are certainly *five* ancient editions, the *first* and *second* of Erasmus, one printed at Hagenau in 1521, another at Strasburg in 1524, and that of Colinæus, in 1534, which have it not; and several more, including the *Editio Princeps*, in which the final clause of the eighth verse is removed from its proper place to eke out the seventh. Instead of *many*, there is not *one* copy which contains the ἐν τῇ γῇ of the eighth verse, whilst destitute of the seventh. So far from not being imaginable, it is both very imaginable and very clear, how the present reading got into the text; which was done first, by inserting the marginal gloss on the eighth verse into the body of some of the Latin manuscripts; and then by the Greek editors translating and re-translating the words from the Latin Vulgate, and inserting them into the printed Greek text. Nor is there any fraud chargeable either on the Arians, or on the orthodox of the fourth and fifth centuries; during whose controversy, and for several ages after, the passage of the *heavenly witnesses* was existing only in the womb of futurity. The real fraud was committed by the Greek editors, who, about three hundred years ago, dared to insert it in their respective editions, contrary to the authority of the Greek manuscripts. Moreover, it is not true, that the words are either distinctly found or alluded to in Tertullian; nor yet in St. Cyprian, if the matter be but duly considered. Neither is it at this day allowed of St. Jerome, whatever it may have been in the time of Dr. Hammond, that he asserted the truth of our reading from his Greek copies; and defended it against all opponents. This argument evidently rests on the false supposition, that the prologue to the Canonical Epistles was written by Jerome; whereas, ever since the Benedictine edition of his works, nearly every scholar and critic of eminence, including your Lordship amongst the number, have been convinced, that it is the composition of some sophisticator of the sixth or seventh century; and fabricated chiefly with the design to procure for the *heavenly witnesses* a place in the Latin Version. But, finally, what advocate of the text is there now to be found to confirm the statement, that St. Ambrose has charged the heretics with the erasure of the passage? In what part of the works of that Father is any such declaration forthcoming; and on what authority has Dr. Hammond made this assertion? Nay, show me the place only where St. Ambrose has taken the least notice of the passage; and I will be ready to acknowledge, that it is not destitute of support, nor unworthy of being vindicated, as a genuine text of Scripture. Alas, this *learned* defence of Dr. Hammond sets all learning at defiance; nor is there so much as one single argument made use of by him, which is not advanced upon grounds palpably mistaken and incorrect." *

In 1707, Dr. Mill published at Oxford his valuable edition of the Greek New Testament, containing at least 30,000 various readings. He admits the disputed passage into his text; but in his prolegomena and notes, he furnishes a mass of evidence, from which it is difficult to understand how he could draw an inference in favor of the passage. So it was, however. As an honest critic, he fairly adduces the evidence

* Oxlee's Letters to the Bishop of Salisbury, pp. 4–7.

on both sides, and furnishes all his readers with data, on which they may either receive or reject his opinion as a divine.

The Abbé L. Roger, Dean of Bourges, published at Paris, in 1715, Two Dissertations; in the first of which he defends 1 John v. 7. "It ought to be mentioned to his credit," says Porson, "that having examined the MSS. in the Royal Library at Paris, he subscribed to the opinion of Lucas Brugensis, Simon, and Le Long, and ingenuously confessed that the semicircle in Stephens's edition, which now follows the words ἐν τῷ οὐρανῷ in the seventh verse, ought to be placed after the words ἐν τῇ γῇ in the eighth." *

After the appearance of Mill's edition, Thomas Emlyn, a Presbyterian minister of Dublin, published "A Full Enquiry into the original Authority of that Text, 1 John v. 7. Containing an Account of Dr. Mill's Evidences from Antiquity, for and against its being genuine. With an Examination of his Judgment thereupon. Humbly addressed to both Houses of Convocation." London, 1715, 1719, 8vo. This is a bold and acute pamphlet; in which the author shows that the passage is wanting in the ancient Greek MSS., the ancient versions, and is never cited by the primitive fathers; and that the other arguments offered in support of the text are insufficient. Whether it was in jest or in earnest that he dedicated his work to the Convocation, I will not take it upon me to say.

Father Simon and Emlyn were taken up by David Martin, Pastor of the French Protestant Church at Utrecht. His work first appeared in French in 1717; and in 1719, it was

* Letters to Travis, Preface, p. v.

translated, though incorrectly, into English, by Dr. Sam. Jebb, with the following title:

"A Critical Dissertation upon the Seventh Verse of the Fifth Chapter of St. John's First Epistle. Wherein the Authentickness of this Text is fully proved against the Objections of Mr. Simon and the Modern Arians." London, 8vo.

Emlyn immediately published "An Answer to Mr. Martin's Critical Dissertation on 1 John v. 7, shewing the Insufficiency of his *Proofs*, and the Errors of his *Suppositions;* by which he attempts to establish the Authority of that Text from *supposed* Manuscripts." London, 1719, 8vo.

Martin, not intimidated, produced, without delay, "An Examination of Mr. Emlyn's Answer to the Dissertation," London, 1719, 8vo; which was closely followed by Emlyn, in a "Reply to Mr. Martin's Examination of the Answer to his Dissertation," London, 1720, 8vo.

Emlyn's pamphlets were first published anonymously; they were afterwards collected, and, with other things, published with his name in 1719, and then in his Works, Vol. II. 1746.

Martin, in another tract, was allowed to have the last word. "The Genuineness of 1 John v. 7. demonstrated by Proofs which are beyond all Exceptions," &c. London, 1722, 8vo.

In this performance he further endeavored to maintain his former positions by the testimony of the Greek and Latin Churches, and particularly by a Greek MS. found in Ireland. Thus the debate rested between these combatants.

Emlyn engaged in this controversy at the request of Dr. Samuel Clarke and Mr. Whiston; the former being too wary of his reputation to appear publicly in a discussion which would have confirmed the suspicion of his Arianism; and the latter not deeming it proper, at the time, to appear on the field. Whiston tells us that both Dr. Bentley and Dr. Waterland approved of Emlyn's view of the subject. Waterland, though so zealous a Trinitarian, never quotes this passage as genuine.

Emlyn was a man of undoubted talents and learning, whose severe and unmerited sufferings, as an Arian, have given considerable celebrity to his name. In his first work on this subject, he professes to give only the evidence as furnished by Dr. Mill, in his critical edition of the New Testament, and his reasons for coming to a different conclusion from that evidence, from that which Mill himself had adopted. His doctrinal sentiments, perhaps, naturally led him to take the strongest view of the side of the question which he espoused, and to rejoice in the strength which it seemed to bring to the Arian cause. But, while the state of his mind predisposed him to give all the weight possible to the evidence against the passage, it would be unfair to charge him with partiality or injustice in the discussion.

In the subsequent tracts which he published, he, of course, followed the steps of his opponent; sometimes strengthening his original position, by adding to the negative evidence against the passage; and at other times exposing the ignorance, the evasions, the false reasonings, and inconclusive arguments of Martin.

Of David Martin it is proper to speak well, as of a man who held sound views of the truth, and was zealously disposed to maintain them. In learning he was very inferior to Simon, and much inferior to Emlyn; though far from being contemptible as a scholar. Considering the materials he had to work with, and the opponents he encountered, it must be confessed that he makes no despicable figure. His mode of treating the subject, however, is more calculated to throw dust in the eyes of his readers than to enlighten and convince them. His judgment was too weak, and his indignation at Arianism too ardent to enable him to do justice to a subject which he treated with all the warmth of a theologian, rather than with the coolness of a critic. It has been boasted, that, in the controversy with Emlyn, he had the last word; and that though Emlyn lived more than twenty years after Martin's last publication, he never attempted to reply. But this needs excite no wonder. Emlyn thought there was no honor to be acquired in "thrice slaying the slain;" and at the close of his second reply thus takes leave of his opponent: — "When a controversy comes to consist only of tedious repetitions, and personal reflections, 'tis a sign it either is near to an end, or ought to be so." If Martin had the honor to be left in possession of the field, it has been thought by many learned men the only honor he obtained.

Dr. Edmund Calamy, one of the most learned divines among the English Dissenters of the period, was the next person who took the field on the affirmative side of this controversy. He published, in 1722, "A Vindication of that celebrated Text, 1 John v. 7, from being spurious; and an Explication of it, upon the supposition of its being genuine. In four Sermons." London. 8vo. These discourses were occasioned by the Arian Controversy, which then so unhappily distracted both the Church and the Dissenters, and are annexed to thirteen sermons on the Doctrine of the Trinity, preached at Salter's Hall in 1719 and 1720. In these four discourses, Dr. Calamy has chiefly in his eye Mr. Emlyn and Father Simon, glancing occasionally at Whiston and some others. The Doctor had no opportunity of examining MSS. himself, and therefore on this part of the subject he reasons entirely on the authority of others; but justice obliges me to state that this authority he does not always allege correctly. The whole controversy is one of fact and evidence; when it comes therefore to be observed that these are not fairly stated, or are dexterously evaded, a suspicion is induced that the cause is not good. It might be inferred from Dr. Calamy's reasonings, that a considerable number of Greek and Latin MSS. and the consent of many Greek and Latin fathers concurred in supporting this text. The contrary had even then been very satisfactorily made out, and is now completely proved.

The best of the four discourses is the last, in which, assuming the testimony to be authentic, he reasons on its nature and design. The Christian reader will cordially concur in his concluding observations. "Since the Father, the Word, and the Holy Ghost are witnesses in order to our confirmation, let us readily believe the truth of whatever they testify, provided we have but good reason to believe that they have testified it, though it seem ever so much to thwart our natural sentiments, or our inclinations. This is a thing that highly becomes such closely dependent, and such dark and dim-sighted creatures as we are; and it is what we cannot have any occasion to be ashamed of. Where Father, Word, and Holy Spirit have gone before, let us readily follow. What light they are pleased to give us, let us thankfully receive, and carefully improve; and from them jointly let us take our measures. And then, if Father, Son, and Holy Spirit can help us to happiness, we need not be apprehensive that we shall miss of it, either in the life that now is, or in that which is to come."

Some time after the publication of Dr. Calamy's Discourses, an anonymous tract appeared on the same side, with the following title: "An Enquiry into the Authority of the

Primitive Complutensian Edition of the New Testament, as principally founded on the most Ancient Vatican Manuscript; together with some Research of that Manuscript. In order to decide the Dispute about 1 John v. 7. In a Letter to the Rev. Mr. Archdeacon Bentley, Master of Trinity College in Cambridge." 1722.

My copy of this pamphlet is contained in Lord Somers's Collection of Tracts,* in which it was reprinted, without mentioning the date of the original edition, or the name of the author.

The writer of this tract was [Richard] Smalbroke, Bishop of Lichfield and Coventry, who distinguished himself both in the Arian Controversy, and in that with Woolston. He was not disposed to adopt the views of Emlyn, nor was he satisfied with the defence of the passage by Martin. Yet he alleges very little that is new on the subject. His whole argument is founded on the supposition, that the Complutensian editors inserted the passage from the Vatican manuscript. Hence, he expresses his strong desire, that this manuscript should be sought out and re-examined. Should it be found not to contain the disputed text, he admits it would confute the reasonings of his essay; but contends, that it still would not follow that the passage was spurious. The following extract contains his argument: —

"Upon the whole, if it shall appear from the Vatican MS. when retriev'd, that the Complutensian editors inserted the disputed passage of St. John from that most ancient copy, an end will be put effectually to the insults of the adversaries of that passage. And if it cannot be discovered, but must be given up for a lost or perish'd copy, yet still the strong probabilities will continue, that the Complutensian editors

* [See Vol. I. pp. 489-506 of the edition of 1748, or Vol. XIII. pp. 458-472, ed 1815. — Ed.]

inserted the said passage from it. However, it is very just and reasonable that the controversy about this passage should be suspended, till the greatest diligence possible be used to find out the celebrated Vatican MS. And then it will be time enough to decide upon the authority of this passage. In the mean time, as the method proposed by yourself, Sir, of endeavoring to find out whether the said passage be genuine or not, by an accurate collation of the most ancient Latin MSS. of the New Testament, as supposed to be translated from the most ancient uncorrupt Greek copies; as this consequential method, I say, is subsidiary, and may contribute to give some new light in this dispute, (though it cannot be allowed to be a decisive argument,) so is it highly probable that it is a method which will be serviceable towards the establishment of this passage of St. John. For far the greater number of those Latin MSS. that have been hitherto collated by learned men, retain this passage; and many of them, no doubt, are very ancient. Whatever be the result of collating your own Latin MSS., asserted by you to be very ancient, the public will be glad to be informed of it. For though it should happen that they want this passage, their authority will not be conclusive against that of a multitude of other very ancient Latin MSS. that are not [Query ?] known to retain it.

"On the other side, if it shall appear from the Vatican MS., when retriev'd, that the Complutensian editors did not insert the disputed passage of St. John from that most ancient copy, but from Latin copies of great antiquity; though such a discovery would confute the reasons assigned in this discourse, yet agreeably to the method proposed by yourself, Sir, of finding out the genuine Greek text by the concurrence of very ancient Latin copies, that were translated from the most ancient and uncorrupt Greek MSS., I say upon this principle, neither the reputation of the Complutensian edition of the Greek Testament, nor the authority of this controverted text in particular, would be affected by such a discovery. For if Stunica and his brethren were persuaded that most, if not all, the Greek MSS. of St. John that are now extant, were corrupted, and that the Latin copies that retain this controverted passage were agreeable to the most ancient uncorrupted Greek copies, and that consequently this passage ought justly to be inserted in that edition, as in fact it was; I do not see why they ought to undergo any censure from yourself, who pay so great a regard to, and lay so mighty a stress upon, the ancient Latin copies of the New Testament, whatever opinion the rest of the learned world might, on this occasion, entertain, by way of diminution, of the authority of the Complutensian editors."

That neither the Vatican MS., nor any other used by the Complutensian editors, contains the passage, has been most satisfactorily proved: consequently the main argument of this pamphlet, by the Bishop's own admission, is overthrown. The other argument, addressed to Dr. Bentley himself, on the *ad hominem* principle, is worth very little. Bentley's edition was never published, so that how the passage might have appeared in it, may be matter of dispute; but that he believed the passage to be spurious is well ascertained, from a discourse which he delivered on the subject, which, it is supposed, is still preserved. A letter also from Bentley to an anonymous friend, shows that his sentiments were understood to be unfavorable to the authority of the verse; and certainly was not intended to remove that unfavorable impression. The execution of his edition of the New Testament on the principle of that letter would undoubtedly have left out the text. As this letter is important, both in reference to this dispute and to the nature of the text of Bentley's intended edition of the New Testament, it is here subjoined.

"Trin. Coll., Jan. 1, 1716-17.

"Sir,—Yours of December the 20th came safely to my hands, wherein you tell me from common fame, that in my designed edition of the New Testament, I purpose to leave out the verse of John's Epistle I. chap. 5. v. 7.

"About a year ago, reflecting upon some passages of St. Hierom, that he had adjusted and castigated the then Latin Vulgate to the best Greek exemplars, and had kept the very order of the words of the original: I formed a thought, *a priori*, that if St. Jerom's true Latin Exemplar could now be come at, it would be found to agree exactly with the Greek text of the same age: and so the old copies of each language (if so agreeing) would give mutual proof, and even demonstration to each other. Whereupon rejecting the printed editions of each, and the several manuscripts of seven centuries and under, I made use of none but those of a thousand years ago or above (of which sort I have twenty now in my study, that one with another make 20,000 years). I had the pleasure to find, as I presaged, that they agreed exactly, like two tallies, or two indentures; and I am able from thence to lead men out of the labyrinth of 60,000 various lections (for St. Jerom's Latin has as many varieties as the Greek), and to give the text as it stood in the best copies in the time of the Council of Nice, without the error of fifty words.

"Now in this work I indulge nothing to any conjecture, not even in a letter, but proceed solely upon authority of copies and fathers of that age. And what will be the event about the said verse of John, I myself know not yet; having not used all the old copies that I have information of.

"But by this you see, that in my proposed work the fate of that verse will be a mere *question of fact*. You endeavor to prove (and that 's all you aspire to) that it *may* have been writ by the Apostle, being consonant to his other doctrine. This I concede to you; and if the fourth century knew that text, let it come in, in God's name: but if that age did not know it, then Arianism in its height was beat down, without the help of that verse: and let the *fact* prove as it will, the *doctrine* is unshaken.

"Yours,

"RIC. BENTLEY."

As, among other things discussed in this controversy, the opinion of Dr. Bentley respecting the authority of this verse has been much debated, it may be proper shortly to advert to it. Porson quotes Bentley as in opposition to the verse, while Bishop Burgess manifests considerable anxiety to secure his suffrage in support of the passage; and Bishop Van Mildert also inclines to doubt respecting Bentley's regarding the passage as spurious.* Nor is it surprising that this concern should be felt to ascertain the opinion of so distinguished a scholar, on a point he was so well qualified to determine. That opinion, if fully formed, would be worth a host of Martins and Travises, men so little qualified to do justice to such an investigation. Crito Cantabrigiensis has set the matter to rest respecting Bentley. After giving some account of the suspicions entertained at the time, that Dr. Bentley's opinion was not in favor of the authenticity of the passage, he thus states the authority on which it can no longer be doubted which side of the question was espoused by that eminent scholar.

"Mr. Whiston, in a letter to a friend (1724), mentions Dr. Bentley 'who read a very learned Lecture at Cambridge, to prove 1 John v. 7. to be spurious.' 'But he dares not now,' continues Whiston, 'wholly omit it in the text of his edition

* Life of Waterland, p. 26.

of the New Testament which he has promised:'—a proof of the jealousy with which Dr. Bentley's proceedings were watched. On another occasion, Mr. Whiston writes to the same effect: 'This treatise (Emlyn's Full Inquiry), as I have been informed, was alluded to by Dr. Bentley in his famous Lecture at Cambridge when he stood candidate for the Chair of Regius Professor of Divinity, wherein he also gave up that text, and publicly proved it to be spurious.' Dr. Middleton, at the very time a resident member of the University, asserts the same thing, as a matter perfectly notorious. 'He (Bentley) has already, *we know*, determined against the genuineness of the famous passage, 1 John v. 7.' Such are the accounts which were delivered by the best informed of Dr. Bentley's contemporaries; and have, till now, been received as true, by persons not at all remarkable for credulity. In what way then are these statements to be set aside? Ancient testimony is opposed by modern argument, after the following fashion. Dr. Bentley observed, in a Letter, that in his intended edition of the New Testament, he should make great use of old Latin MSS.; that, not having seen all the old copies he had information of, he knew not at that time what would be the fate of the text in question: and that if he found the text to have existed in the fourth century, he would admit it. And thus, because Dr. Bentley, in this letter, gave no opinion touching the verse, and attributed great importance to the old Latin MSS., it is inferred that if he 'read a Lecture to prove this verse spurious,' 'the Lecture and the Letter must have been very much at variance.' Now, in answer to all this, I would humbly suggest three things: 1. That a person who will not decide a question before inquiry is by no means incompetent to do so afterwards: 2. That, as the Letter was written on the first of January, and the Lecture delivered about the first of May following, Dr. Bentley may have examined his MSS. and made up his mind during the interval: and, 3. That as we know not *how* Dr. Bentley *reasoned*, we ought to receive the conclusion at which he arrived on the information of his contemporaries. In truth, take the argument above mentioned as an argument upon a mere hypothetical case, and its weakness is excessive; but consider its conclusion as in direct opposition to a fact stated on evidence, and it disappears, like a bubble, the instant it is touched. . . . . For the purpose of ascertaining the tendency of a Lecture read in 1717, I must be excused for trusting to the testimony of Conyers Middleton — who lived on the spot at the time when the Lecture was delivered — in preference to the most ingenious conjectures of the present day, although sanctioned by the high authority of the Bishops of Durham and Salisbury." *

The first edition of the Greek New Testament published in England, which omits the passage, appeared in 1729.

* Crito Cantab. pp. 154-158. [Bp. Monk, in his Life of Bentley, (London, 1830, pp. 349-351,) has placed the fact of Bentley's rejection of the passage beyond the possibility of dispute. Referring to the letter of January 1, 1717, quoted above, he states that "Bentley, finding how much the question interested the public mind, and perceiving that there was expected from the editor of the New Testament a clear expression of opinion on this point, applied himself in the course of the four following months to examine all the evidence on both sides. Having chosen this as the subject of his Prælection, he gave a regular history of the verse, and an account of the manner in which the passage of St. John is quoted by ancient writers; and concluded with a decided rejection of the verse; maintaining at the same time the doctrine of the Trinity in its orthodox acceptation, and showing that it stood not in any need of such dubious support." After citing the testimony of those who had heard the Lecture, he adds: "Dr. Vincent, the late learned Dean of Westminster, had once the original of this piece in his possession, lent to him by a relative of Bentley: a letter of his now lies before me, containing the account of the contents which I have just given, and adding, that to him 'it was conviction.'"—Ed.]

"The New Testament in Greek and English. Containing the Original Text corrected from the Authority of the most Authentic Manuscripts: and a new Version form'd agreeably to the Illustrations of the most learned Commentators and Critics: with Notes and various Readings." London, 2 vols., 8vo.

The editor and translator of this work was Dr. Mace, of whose history very little is known, but that he belonged to the free school of theology. The Greek text is beautifully printed, but its authority as a critical edition does not stand high, as the editor appears to have been a rash and a vain man, who took very unwarrantable liberties with the text, and seldom assigns satisfactory reasons for the alterations, which he made with much freedom. Indeed, his object seems to have been to throw a degree of uncertainty over the whole text and canonical authority of the New Testament. On the disputed verse, however, he enters at some length. He gives a list of Greek MSS. in which it is not to be found; of Latin MSS. in which it is omitted; of Greek fathers who do not notice it; of Latin writers in the first five centuries who do not mention it; and of printed editions which want it. He then notices the Greek and Latin authorities which are supposed to be in its favor. He concludes his examination and comparison by exclaiming: "In a word, if this evidence is not sufficient to prove that the controverted text in St. John is *spurious*, by what evidence can it be prov'd that any text in St. John is genuine? The authority upon which any Greek text is founded, is only the authority of the Greek fathers, and their authority is founded upon that of the antient Greek MSS. Now ALL the Greek fathers, *not one* excepted; ALL the Greek MSS., the *Irish one* only excepted; ALL the antient Versions, the old Italic and St. Jerom's, the Syriac, the Æthiopic, the Arabic, and the Coptic; ALL the antient Latin fathers, and the most antient Latin MSS. of the New Testament, do unanimously exclaim against the controverted text." *

The publication of this work led to the following: — "A Critical Examination of the late New Text and Version of the New Testament: wherein the Editor's corrupt Text, false Version, and fallacious Notes are detected and censured. By Leonard Twells, Vicar of St. Mary's. In Three Parts. In the Second of which Justice is done to the famous Text of 1 John v. 7, against his partial Representation of that Matter." London, 1731.

Twells, the author of this examination, was a clergyman of the Church of England, not very distinguished for the accuracy of his researches or the extent of his learning. It was no hard task to expose the incorrectness of Mace's text, and the blunders and absurdities of his translation. But in attacking his omission of the disputed passage in John, Twells had not Mace, but Mill's authorities to contend with. In doing this, he flounders in the darkness of his own misconceptions, hazards the most groundless assumptions, and dogmatically asserts what had been repeatedly disproved. He concludes a long discussion by a passage precisely the opposite of that quoted from Mace, in the latter part of which, it must be acknowledged, he has a just stroke at that rash and vulgar critic: "The disputed passage of 1 John v. 7, has so many marks of genuineness, that if it had not contained a doctrine, to which the disputers of this world have always shown the utmost aversion, its authority had never been called in question. An undoubted proof of which is this, that many texts of Scripture, according to their present reading, are worse supported than this, and yet receive no molestation from critics. And of all others, the editor should

* Vol. II. p. 934.

be the last to object to the disputed passage, as defective in point of testimony, who admits some lections into his new text upon the credit of simple vouchers, and others against all authority whatever." (p. 154.)

David Casley published, in 1734, "A Catalogue of the MSS. of the King's Library, together with 150 specimens of the manner of writing in different ages, from the third to the fifteenth century." In his preface to this Catalogue, he refers to the controversy respecting the heavenly witnesses, and gives his opinion, that the Codex Britannicus is "a modern MS. probably translated, or corrected, from the Latin Vulgate."

Bengelius published his valuable critical edition of the Greek Testament in 1734; in which the principles on which he constructed his text led him to insert the passage. He adopted no reading which had not previously appeared in some printed edition, except in some cases in the Apocalypse. In consequence of following a law, which he had laid down for himself, more specious and better adapted to meet the popular feeling on certain points than solid in itself, he admitted the passage; and yet the statements in his note seem fatal to its authority. He allows that it exists in no genuine manuscript; that the Complutensian editors interpolated it from the Latin version; that the Codex Britannicus is good for nothing; that Stephens's semicircle is misplaced; that no ancient Greek writer cites the heavenly witnesses; that many Latins omit them; that they were neither erased by the Arians, nor absorbed by the *homœoteleuton*. He thought the evidence afforded by the African Church, and some other considerations, favorable to the passage, and therefore inserted it, but, on the whole, he had no strong conviction of its authenticity.

As a good deal, however, has been said of the weight of Bengel's opinion, the following view of his conduct in this matter seems to be characterized by great accuracy and candor. "Bengelius was, probably, the first advocate of the verse who fairly gave up the notion that the Complutensian editors and Robert Stephens printed the passage as they found it in Greek MSS. He also allowed due weight to the silence of the fathers with regard to the text. In fact, he was a good workman; and, in the progress of his undertaking, he cleared the subject of many incumbrances. He condemned the principle of defending a text because it favored a particular doctrine. He disdained to measure a person's orthodoxy by his reception of the text of the heavenly witnesses. He contended that the great object of inquiry was, whether what was held to have been written really had been written. He censured the mode in which the verse had, in many instances, been defended; and even mentioned its great champion, Dr. Twells himself, with no great reverence. Towards the close of his inquiry, he seems to have considered the subject as one on which learned men might justly hold opposite opinions; and in his Greek Testament he stated his wish, that the reader should suppose, as his own judgment might direct, either the seventh verse to be erased, or the eighth verse to precede the seventh; for his own part recommending the latter supposition. This mode of proceeding was anything but agreeable to those who were resolved that the text should be vindicated, at all events. In literary campaigns, the established rule seems to be, that he who first deserts a position as untenable, however valiantly he may fight in other instances, shall be accounted as little better than one of the enemy; and accordingly, Bengelius was, more than once, obliged to defend himself from the charge of indifference to the cause in which he was engaged. 'In vain,' says

Mr. Porson, 'may Simon, La Croze, Michaelis, and Griesbach, declare their belief of the doctrine [of the Trinity]; they must defend it in the Catholic manner, and with the Catholic texts: nor is all this enough: but, in defending the genuineness of a particular text, they must use every one of the same arguments that have already been used, without rejecting any upon the idle pretence that they are false or trifling. I pity Bengelius. He had the weakness, which fools call candor, to reject some of the arguments that had been employed in defence of this celebrated verse, and brought upon himself a severe, but just rebuke from an opposer of De Missy (Journ. Brit., X. 133); where he is ranked with those 'who, under pretext of defending the three heavenly witnesses with moderation, defend them so gently that a suspicious reader might doubt whether they defended them in earnest; though God forbid that we should wish to insinuate any suspicion of Mr. Bengelius's orthodoxy.' " *

In 1734, a volume of discourses on the disputed passage was published, with the following title: "The Doctrine of the Trinity, as it is contained in the Scriptures, explained and confirmed: its Consistency with the Principles of Natural Religion cleared, and Objections to the Contrary answered, &c." The author of these discourses was the Rev. James Sloss, M. A., a dissenting minister of the Independent denomination at Nottingham. He seems to have been a man of respectable attainments as a scholar; and defends the doctrine of the Trinity with considerable ability, though not always with those arguments which will stand the test of a critical examination. Of this his choice of the disputed passage for the text of the whole eighteen sermons is an illus-

* Crito Cantabrigiensis, pp. 311-314. [Porson's Letters to Travis, pp. 18-20. — Ed.]

tration. With his general views or defence of the doctrine of the Trinity, however, I have at present nothing to do. Our business is with his account of the testimony of the heavenly witnesses. Dr. Burgess, who seems to have collected every name and authority bearing on his side of the question, seems to have known nothing of James Sloss. This will be my excuse for noticing him more particularly.

In the first sermon he engages "to trace the several ages between this and the apostles, and to show how this text in particular has been owned as authentic by the whole Christian Church, both Greek and Latin." Had he succeeded in this attempt, we should never have heard of the sneers of Gibbon, nor been favored with the debates of Travis and Porson. But, alas! the words we have quoted, big with promise, end in miserable disappointment. He quotes the usual passages from Tertullian, Cyprian, Eucherius, Vigilius Tapsensis, Eugenius, Fulgentius, &c., &c., and accordingly arrives at his conclusion with great apparent ease, that the passage has been disputed only by Arians and Socinians.

The discourses appear to have attracted some attention, as they led to an epistolary controversy respecting the authority of the text, which is printed at the end of the book. A gentleman, whose name is only given as the Rev. T. P., of C——l, addressed a letter to Mr. Sloss, stating to him the doubts which he entertained about this passage, and the general grounds of those doubts, and requesting his solution of them. The letter is written very calmly and respectfully, and shows that the writer of it knew very well the subject on which he requests information. To this Mr. Sloss replies in a letter of considerable length, which contains some acute observations on the doctrine of the Trinity, but utterly fails in giving the information on certain matters of fact respecting the authenticity of the disputed verse. This his antagonist notices in a second letter to Mr. Sloss, which produced two in reply. These were followed by another short epistle from T. P., demanding whether Mr. Sloss knew "of any other *Greek* manuscripts, beside that of Dublin, now in being, with the disputed verse in it; and, secondly, whether he could prove that any editor of the printed copies ever had any such MSS. in his possession." To this Mr. Sloss returned a final answer, but which does not contain the information wanted. Here the debate closed. The parties seem to have been matched nearly as Emlyn and Martin were. Sloss was, like Martin, an orthodox Trinitarian, and his correspondent was evidently of the school of Emlyn. In learning and knowledge of the subject, however, both Sloss and his opponent were inferior to the two former controversialists. The letters occupy seventy-eight pages.

In the critical edition of the New Testament published by Wetstein in 1752, the passage is marked as spurious. There is also attached to it a long and important note, in which the mark is justified by a reference to a much greater number of MSS. and versions than had ever before been quoted in the controversy. The leaning of Wetstein's mind to the Unitarian hypothesis is well known, and has excited a suspicion that he may have been influenced by it in his rejection of this passage. This is scarcely candid, as he states fairly and fully the evidence on which he formed his decision.

Part of the note, which contains Stephens's account of the use he made of his MSS., and of his mode of referring to them, with Wetstein's strictures on that account, it may be useful to quote.

"In his preface to the third edition, Stephens says, 'In the inner margin I have added various readings of the MSS., to each whereof the mark of the Greek numeral is subjoined, which indicates the name of the MS. whence it is taken; or of the MSS. when they are many. And I have put the marks in succession from one to sixteen: so that the first stands for the Complutensian edition; the second, for the most ancient MS. in Italy, collated by my friends; the third, fourth, fifth, sixth, seventh, eighth, tenth, and fifteenth, the copies which I had out of the King's Library; the others are those which I was able to collect from all quarters.'

" *To this account of things by R. Stephens, and of his own great care and diligence, I have much to object*," says Wetstein; "first, what this very edition of Stephens plainly shows, that the editor has varied from all his MSS. and introduced a different reading, not only where he has marked in his margin that a different reading from that which he adopted was found in all the MSS.; but often when otherwise. Add to this, that his second edition, though it has the same preface which is prefixed to the first, yet varies from it in fifty places at the least.

" Secondly, I would observe, that Stephens had not the use of sixteen MSS. of the First Epistle of John, but only of seven. The first copy he made use of was not a MS., but the Complutensian edition of the N. T. The second, which is now the Cambridge MS., contains only the Gospels and the Acts. The third contains only the four Gospels, and is now to be seen in the King of France's Library, marked 2867. Also the sixth, in the King's Library, No. 2866. The eighth, ditto, 2861. The twelfth, ditto, 2862, and the fourteenth, ditto, 2865. Lastly, the sixteenth is cited by Stephens only in the Revelation. There is indeed a various reading of 2 Pet. i. 4, produced from the fourteenth MS.; but as that MS. is still in the King's Library, and contains the Gospels only, it must have been a mistake of the compositors. Which kind of mistakes occurs elsewhere, and much more frequently in this edition of Stephens's than is commonly imagined. This any one will readily find, who compares the Complutensian edition with the various readings from it noted down by Stephens.

"But, thirdly, what above all is to be noted, the inspection of Stephens's MSS., and ocular demonstration show, not only that in those MSS. the words *in heaven*, but all that follow so far as to *the spirit* in the 8th verse, are wanting [viz. the words *in heaven, the Father, the Word, and the Holy Spirit: and these three are one. And there are three that bear witness in earth*], so that Stephens's semicircle, which should have been put after the words *in earth* (to mark the whole of what was wanting, as it is put in his Latin editions), was placed after the words *in heaven*, by the fault of the compositors. This Lucas Brugensis had suspected to be the case; but Father Simon, Le Long, and L. Roger have clearly demonstrated it. Consult the MSS. in the King's Library; the 2871st, which is Stephens's fourth; the 3425th, which is his fifth; the 2242d, which is Stephens's seventh; the 2869th, Stephens's fifteenth (which however he never seems to have collated in the Epistles), 2870th, Stephens's tenth, and Coislinianus 200, Stephens's ninth; and it will be manifest to every one, as it was to me who inspected these MSS. after those three eminent persons just named, that the whole of that verse of the *three heavenly witnesses* was certainly wanting in five of Stephens's MSS. of the Catholic Epistles. As to his two other MSS., as they have never yet been found, there is no determining about them.

"This mistake of the compositor," proceeds Wetstein, "led Beza wrong: who gives this note upon the place, in his first and second editions. '*This* (*7th*) *verse seems to me by all means to be retained:— Erasmus reads it so in a British MS. I also have read it in some of our Robert's* (Stephens) *ancient*

*MSS.*' Which is not to be understood, as if Beza with his own eyes had seen those MSS., for how could it be, when Stephens had left them behind him at Paris? but that he made use of Stephens's third edition for the purpose. But it may be said, that Stephens ought to have informed his friend Beza of the mistake of the compositor, and should not have suffered, that through this first edition of Beza, printed with Stephens's types, and the editions that followed, a mistake in so serious and important a point should have been propagated far and near. I confess there is a great deal in this remark. But perhaps Stephens neglected to inform him of it: or, how shall we ascertain, whether Beza's note was approved or disliked by Stephens?"

Soon after the publication of this important work, several letters appeared against Martin and the disputed passage, in the Journal Britannique.* They were written by César de Missy, a native of Berlin, French preacher in the Savoy, and at St. James's. They discovered great learning and penetration, but were written, for the most part, in rather too ludicrous a tone for serious criticism. In these letters were particularly exposed the ridiculous and false pretence of Amelotte, that the disputed passage was contained in a Vatican MS., and the absurd inference which some persons had deduced from Wetstein's correction of an erratum relative to the three lectionaries belonging to César de Missy; this correction having been converted into an acknowledgment, that the passage was contained in one of these three lectionaries.† "De Missy's fate," says Porson, "has been somewhat hard. He was bold enough to attack Amelotte's veracity and Martin's understanding. This provoked a nest of hornets. Four

* [Tomes VIII. and IX., 1752.—Ed.]

† Marsh's Michaelis, Vol. VI. p. 414.

anonymous writers fell upon him; three with personal abuse, the fourth with malignity, under the mask of moderation." *

Nothing more of importance on the subject occurred till 1754, when "Two Letters of Sir Isaac Newton to Mr. Le Clerc, upon the reading of the Greek text, 1 John v. 7 and 1 Tim. iii. 16," appeared. They had been drawn up by Sir Isaac so early as the beginning of the century, and were at last published from the MSS. left by Le Clerc in the Library of the Remonstrants in Amsterdam. The first Letter is entirely devoted to the text of the heavenly witnesses. The first four pages of the MS. being lost, the beginning is supplied by the editor, whose name does not appear. The MS. was sent to Le Clerc by Mr. Locke, and is said to have been in his handwriting. It is almost entirely occupied with a history of what Sir Isaac considered the manner in which the testimony came to be surreptitiously inserted, first into the Latin MSS., and then into the printed Greek text. Some of his remarks bear very hard upon Beza, whom he calls a dreamer, and almost justify the sneers of Gibbon. Sir Isaac assigns several reasons for believing that the Complutensian editors translated the passage from the Latin Vulgate. And, certainly, the marginal note attached to the passage in the Complutensian edition, a practice which is adopted in that edition only in two other places where the Greek MSS. are defective, and the silence of Stunica, one of the editors, in his controversy with Erasmus on the authority of Greek MSS., are strong negative proofs that the passage was translated from the Vulgate. Sir Isaac also endeavors to explain the passage and its context without the three heavenly witnesses. He considers the spirit, the water, and the blood, to mean the promised spirit, the baptism of Christ, and his

* Letters to Travis, p. 19.

passion, in connection with his resurrection, all bearing testimony to his character and mission as the Son of God.

The attention which this eminent man paid to biblical subjects must have been very considerable. The present tract discovers a good deal of critical reading, which, considering his circumstances and pursuits, would not have taken place, had his taste for the Scriptures not been cultivated. His leanings to Arianism, which were no doubt promoted by his acquaintance with Clarke, Whiston, and other eminent persons of that school, are to be deplored. But his character presents a noble contrast to that ruthless infidelity, or cheerless scepticism, which characterize men infinitely his inferiors in all the attainments of genuine philosophy.

I cannot withhold from the reader, as Sir Isaac's tract is not in many hands, his paraphrase of the verses in which the words alleged to be spurious have been inserted. It is, at least, a plausible interpretation of a very difficult passage.

"*Who is he that overcometh the world, but he that believeth that Jesus is the Son of God;* that Son spoken of in the Psalms, where he saith, 'Thou art my Son, this day have I begotten thee.' *This is He that,* after the Jews had long expected him, *came,* first in a mortal body, *by* baptism of *water, and* then in an immortal one, by shedding his *blood* upon the cross, and rising again from the dead; *not by water only, but by water and blood*; being the Son of God, as well by his resurrection from the dead (Acts xiii. 33) as by his supernatural birth of the Virgin. (Luke i. 35.) *And it is the Spirit* also, *that,* together with the water and blood, *beareth witness* of the truth of his coming; *because the Spirit is truth;* and so a fit and unexceptionable witness.

"*For there are three that bear record* of his coming: *the Spirit,* which he promised to send, and which was since shed forth upon us in the form of cloven tongues, and in various gifts; *the* baptism of *water*, wherein God testified, 'This is my beloved Son'; *and the* shedding of his *blood*, accompanied with his resurrection, whereby he became the most faithful martyr, or witness, of this truth. *And these three*, the Spirit, the baptism, and passion of Christ, *agree in* witnessing *one* and the same thing, (namely, that the Son of God is come,) and therefore their evidence is strong: for the law requires but two consenting witnesses, and here we have three: *and if we receive the witness of men, the* threefold *witness of God*, which he bare of his Son, by declaring at his baptism, 'This is my beloved Son'; by raising him from the dead, and by pouring out his Spirit on us, *is greater*, and therefore ought to be more readily received.

"This [Thus?] is the sense plain and natural, and the argument full and strong; but, if you insert the testimony of 'the three in heaven,' you interrupt and spoil it. For the whole design of the Apostle being here to prove to men, by witness, the truth of Christ's coming, I would ask, how the testimony of 'the three in heaven' makes to this purpose. If their testimony be not given to men, how does it prove to them the truth of Christ's coming? If it be, how is the testimony in heaven distinguished from that on earth? It is the same Spirit which witnesses in heaven and in earth. If in both cases it witnesses to us men wherein lies the difference between its witnessing in heaven, and its witnessing in earth? If, in the first case, it does not witness to men, to whom doth it witness? And to what purpose? And how does its witnessing make to the design of St. John's discourse? Let them make good sense of it who are able. For my part, I can make none." *

* Newton's Letters to Le Clerc, pp. 74-76. [This tract was published more correctly in Vol. V. of Horsley's edition of Newton's Works (London, 1785, 4to), under the title, "An Historical Account of Two Notable

In 1756, the second edition of Dr. Benson's work on the Catholic Epistles was published.* In the second volume of this learned and valuable Commentary, there is a Dissertation "Concerning the Genuineness of 1 John v. 7, 8." Dr. Benson, as might be expected, took decided part against the reading. His Dissertation does not contain much that is original; but gives a very lucid view of the substance of the evidence on which Dr. Benson formed his opinion. He begins with the fathers, and shows, that while Tertullian, Cyprian, and Jerome have been referred to, no satisfactory evidence exists in their writings that any of them had read this passage. He next notices the Greek MSS., and alleges that they furnish no authority for the insertion of the passage. The ancient versions, he maintains, are all on the same side. The evidence against the text is next produced, and "the sum of the whole matter" is thus given by the Doctor, in the way of accounting for the introduction of the passage.

"To sum up the whole matter. The true state of the case seems to have been this: As these words were not written by St. John himself, they were not in any ancient MS. or Version, nor known to any of the ancient fathers. But Tertullian applying these words of ver. 8 (These three are one) to Father, Son, and Holy Spirit, Cyprian took that for the mystical interpretation of ver. 8. By him, Facundus, Eucherius, Fulgentius, Austin, and others, were led into that interpretation. And, very probably, Cyprian himself, or

Corruptions of Scripture. In a Letter to a Friend. Now first published entire from a MS. in the Author's handwriting in the possession of the Rev. Dr. Ekens, Dean of Carlisle." It was reprinted in Sparks's "Collection of Essays and Tracts in Theology," Vol. II. (Boston, 1823), and in a separate volume, London, 1830, 8vo. The quotation given above is conformed to the text in Horsley's edition. — Ed.]

* Mr. Butler strangely characterises this work as "a Paraphrase of the Gospels." See Horæ Bib. I. p. 378.

rather some of his admirers, wrote that interpretation in the margin, over-against ver. 8, as a gloss. And by some future transcriber it was incorporated into the text itself.

"There are, at this day, several MSS., both Greek and Latin, which have it in the margin. And such insertions of explanatory words, or phrases, from the margin, into the text, are common in MSS. Jerome, in one of his letters, says, that an explanatory note, which he himself had made in the margin of his psalter, had been incorporated by some transcriber into the text. And Dr. Mill points out many similar instances.

"The English Polyglot, and six other editions of the Syriac New Testament, inform us that the Syriac Version has not the seventh verse. Tremellius likewise observes the same thing. But in a marginal note, he has translated the seventh verse into Syriac; though he dared not insert it into the text in his edition. However, Gutbirius inserted it, contrary to the authority of all the Syriac copies, both printed and manuscript. And, after him, Schaaf, without the authority of one MS. copy of the New Testament in Syriac, hath likewise, in his edition of the Syriac New Testament, boldly, without any apology, and without any mark of distinction, inserted Tremellius his translation into the text. Thus we see by what steps it might be at first brought into the text. Some zealous men have called it a *grand forgery.* And Gutbirius and Schaaf cannot easily be excused. But it is possible that the transcriber who first inserted it in the text might apprehend, that, as he found it interlined, or in the margin, it had been omitted by the former copyist; and that, therefore, he did well in supplying that omission. Others, again, copied after him. And thus it got into some few (but not into the generality) of Latin copies. From those Latin copies, or quotations from thence, it was very probably translated into Greek, and inserted into the text in some modern manuscripts, and interlined, or put in the margin of MSS. of an older date, — as it is now found to be in several MSS., Greek and Latin, in both public and private libraries.

"To make it spread, some busybody, about the eighth or ninth century, by a pious fraud, forged the preface to the Catholic Epistles, under the name of Jerome. And to give it the authority of antiquity, ascribed the restoring of this disputed text, in the *Latin* copies, to that learned father; at the same time complaining of the unfaithfulness of the Latin translators for leaving it out. From thence it appears, that when that preface was forged, the disputed text was in very few Latin copies. But such a preface, under the name of Jerome, would induce many for the future to insert it.

"Thus it may be accounted for why it is not found in the ancient Greek MSS. or the ancient versions; why it is not quoted by the primitive fathers; why it appears more early in the Latin than in the Greek MSS.; and how it comes to be in our printed copies at this day." *

In the second edition of Bowyer's Conjectures on the New Testament, 4to, 1784, there is a note of some length on the passage, which shows that the opinions of the learned printer were unfavorable to its authority. All the reasons which he assigns are adduced at greater length by one or other of the writers in the controversy, and therefore do not require to be distinctly noticed.

We now come to the grand controversy on this important passage, which originated in the following paragraph in Gibbon's "History of the Decline and Fall of the Roman Empire." Speaking of the Catholic frauds, he says, "The

* Benson's Paraphrase, Vol. II. pp. 644–646, 2d edit.

memorable text which asserts the unity of the THREE who bear witness in heaven, is condemned by the universal silence of the orthodox fathers, ancient versions, and authentic MSS. It was first alleged by the Catholic Bishops whom Hunneric summoned to the Conference of Carthage. An allegorical interpretation, in the form, perhaps, of a marginal note, invaded the text of the Latin Bibles, which were renewed and corrected in a dark period of ten centuries. After the invention of printing, the editors of the Greek Testament yielded to their own prejudices, or those of the times; and the pious fraud, which was embraced with equal zeal at Rome and at Geneva, has been infinitely multiplied in every country and every language of modern Europe." In a note to part of this passage, he adds, "The three witnesses have been established in our Greek Testaments by the prudence of Erasmus; the honest bigotry of the Complutensian editors; the typographical fraud, or error, of Robert Stephens, in the placing a crotchet; and the deliberate falsehood, or strange misapprehension, of Theodore Beza."*

On this last sentence volumes of curious and angry controversy have been written. It shows how closely Gibbon had looked into the matter, while the choice of his epithets at once illustrates his knowledge of the subject, and the delight he took in reproaching the professors of Christianity. The infidelity of the writer is ill-disguised in the studied ambiguity of his phraseology, which insinuates that the doctrine of the Trinity is established by worldly prudence, bigotry, fraud, or misapprehension. He well knew that this was not the case. But that prejudiced enemy to Christianity was ever regardless of decency and justice, where its claims and its character were concerned. "He often makes, when he cannot readily find, an occasion to insult our religion, which

* Rom. Emp., Ch. XXXVII. Vol. VI. pp. 291-293, Ed. 1807.

he hates so cordially, that he might seem to revenge some personal injury. Such is his eagerness in the cause, that he stoops to the most despicable pun, or to the most awkward perversion of language, for the pleasure of turning the Scripture into ribaldry, or of calling Jesus an impostor." *

Had the Decline and Fall of the Roman Empire, however, contained nothing more injurious to the doctrine or revelation of the Scriptures, this statement, and the insinuation implied in it, might have been allowed to pass. Like many other things of a similar nature, it would have silently floated down the current of time, and would soon have been lost in that oblivion to which all accusations against the Word of God are doomed. But, unfortunately, Gibbon had a name, and his works enjoyed celebrity. It was the fashion of the day to write apologies for the Bible; and some men who would never have risen to public notice otherwise, endeavored to write themselves into fame or preferment by attacking the infidel historian.

In an evil hour, and prompted by some evil genius, the Rev. George Travis, Archdeacon of Chester, took up his pen, to defend, not the doctrine of the Trinity, but the testimony of the heavenly witnesses, against the charges preferred in the above passage. He addressed three letters to Mr. Gibbon on this subject, in the Gentleman's Magazine for 1782. These he reprinted separately, along with two more, in a quarto volume, in 1784. In 1786, they appeared again with additions. In the same Magazine for 1788 and 1789, Professor Porson replied to Travis. In 1790, Travis wrote another letter on the subject, in the same Magazine, to which Porson replied in the following month. And in 1794, the Archdeacon published the whole, in a large octavo volume.

* Porson's Letters to Travis, Pref., pp. xxviii., xxix.

This is the best edition, and which has been consulted in writing these observations.

In these letters, it is the object of the writer to defend Erasmus, the Complutensian editors, Beza, and Stephens, against Mr. Gibbon's charges; to maintain the authenticity of the disputed passage; to reply seriatim to the leading writers who had disputed it; and to account for its omission from so many MSS. and versions. That Travis undertook a herculean task is very evident; that he sunk under it, can excite no surprise. What he wanted in argument he made up by boldness; and contrived to maintain an appearance of truth and victory, by carefully avoiding to meet his enemy in the face.

He succeeds in defending the first editors of the Greek New Testament against the base insinuations of Gibbon; for though the cause must be given against Mr. Archdeacon Travis, no one will concede to the historian of the Roman Empire, that the learned editors were bigots, hypocrites, or fools. But when, from defending their character, he proceeds to defend their text, the ground becomes very different, and the tactics entirely of another order. Instead of pursuing a straightforward course, in order to reach his point, he is obliged to follow one the most indirect and circuitous. In place of beginning at the beginning, he begins at the end. He commences with the writers and authorities next to the period of the Reformation, and endeavors to trace the stream up to the fountain head. Instead of the evidence becoming clearer and stronger, however, it becomes the feebler and more obscure the longer he pursues it; till, at last, notwithstanding his perpetual mistakes and misstatements, it is left in uncertainty and darkness. His account of the testimony of the writers whom he quotes in support of the passage is, in many instances, not to be depended on, as it is often quoted at second-hand, or some circumstance is left out of view, which, when understood, either in a great measure or entirely subverts it. His account of the MSS. of Valla and Stephens is altogether erroneous; and the impression which he labors to produce, that a great number of Greek and Latin MSS. contain the verse, is directly the reverse of the truth.

He makes a show, for it is often little better, of replying to *fifty-five* arguments or objections of Dr. Benson; and pronounces that his Dissertation, "for intrepidity of assertion, disingenuousness of quotation, and defectiveness of conclusion, has no equal, stands aloof beyond all parallel — as far as his reading extends — either in ancient or in modern times." This is something like the ass kicking the dead lion; but which, as we shall find, was destined to receive no ordinary correction. The character given to Dr. Benson's work, in the opinion of Porson, more properly belongs to the production of Travis. In the same manner, he professes to meet fifty-one arguments of Sir Isaac Newton; whose arguments were not more powerful than Benson's, but who is treated with more courtesy than the Presbyterian divine. Griesbach and Bowyer are dispatched in a very few pages, and not more satisfactorily than the former.

In short, Archdeacon Travis, though a very respectable clergyman, and an able "tythe-lawyer," was altogether disqualified by his prejudices, his ignorance, and his injudiciousness, from rendering any important service to the cause of theological literature, in this important controversy. His own summing up, in the following passage, will show the nature of many of his proofs, or rather assumptions, and the high tone of confidence with which he claims the victory.

"The result, then, from the whole is, — that THE VERSE in question SEEMS, BEYOND ALL DEGREE OF SERIOUS DOUBT, TO HAVE STOOD IN THIS EPISTLE WHEN IT ORIGINALLY

PROCEEDED FROM THE PEN OF ST. JOHN.* In the Latin, or Western Church, the suffrages of Tertullian and Cyprian, of Marcus Celedensis and Phæbadius, in its favor, aided by the early, the solemn, the public appeal to its authority by the African Bishops under Huneric; the Preface, Bible, and *conscripta fides* of Jerome; the frequent and direct citations of the verse by Eucherius, Fulgentius, Vigilius, and Cassiodorius:—these, supported as to the Greek, or Eastern Churches, by the Dialogue imputed to Arius and Athanasius, as well as by the Synopsis of this Epistle; by the Armenian Version, which was framed from Greek MSS.; by the very early and constant use of the αποστολος in the same Greek Church, (an usage which seems to be deducible even from the Apostles themselves,) and by its public Confession of Faith:—all these evidences, arising within the limit of the sixth century (to pass over the immense accumulation of testimony which has been produced subsequent to that era), offering themselves to the test of the judgment, combined in one point of view, unchecked by a single negation, unrebuked by any positive contradiction, unresisted by any the smallest direct impeachment of the authenticity of the verse, throughout all the annals of all antiquity:—ALL THESE CIRCUMSTANCES seize the mind as it were by violence, and compel it to acknowledge the verity, the original existence of the verse in question. For although it undoubtedly appears strange, on a first consideration of the subject, that several ancient Greek and Latin Fathers have not quoted, or commented upon this verse, in those *parts* of their works which have descended to the present age; although it appears, on a primary view, still more strange, that those numerous Greek MSS. (not Latin, for a vast majority of these have *always* read the verse,) which formerly exhibited this pas-

* The capitals are Travis's.

sage of St. John, should be *now* in general (not totally) lost, rather than those few which did not contain it: yet both these objections, when aggravated to the utmost, are but *presumptions*, amount to no more than negative evidence; and they have been already, as it should seem, completely and satisfactorily explained and avoided, or accounted for and defeated. And from whethersoever of the sources, which have been heretofore assigned, the partial occultation of this verse, antecedent to the times of Jerome, proceeded, that temporary obscuration was dispersed at once, and the verse was summoned forth to shine in its proper sphere, by his Preface and Version; which are confirmed and established (if they could be said to need any confirmation or establishment) by the revision of Alcuinus under the direction of Charlemagne. And this verse hath EVER SINCE (if we may now descend to modern times) not only maintained its place in every public version which hath been in use since the days of Jerome; but it hath also been ever since uniformly quoted, and referred to by individual writers of the first eminence for learning and integrity, in Asia and in Africa, as well as in Europe, without the least question, without the smallest interruption, EXCEPT the invasion of Erasmus, which, however, was soon repelled, and of which he frequently repented and was ashamed, unless his own paraphrase on this verse, and his *Ratio Veræ Theologiæ*, be the completest pieces of literary hypocrisy now subsisting; — and, except the assaults of some more modern objectors, which, nevertheless, it is hoped and trusted, have been repulsed in the preceding Dissertation, in a manner, although unequal to the subject, yet sufficiently adequate to the serious conviction of every unprejudiced inquirer after truth." *

Inaccurate and unsatisfactory to scholars as were the Let-

* Pages 455 - 459.

ters of Travis, they produced, when published, a considerable impression. "Nor is it difficult to account for their success. The insidious speculations on religion, which distinguished the History of the Decline and Fall of the Roman Empire, made that work an object of intense interest to the literary public. The principles avowed in the first volume called forth adversaries in abundance; and the author, notwithstanding his cool and philosophical temperament, was at last instigated to take up arms in his own defence. Hostilities against the first volume had scarcely begun to abate, when the publication of the second and third furnished grounds for new engagements. Mr. Travis very adroitly availed himself of the opportunity that was presented, and thus obtained a degree of consequence as the opponent of Mr. Gibbon, which he could not have obtained as the mere advocate of the controverted text. There was besides, in the mode of conducting his attack, much that was very likely to impose upon the generality of mankind. He proclaimed himself the champion of the great cause of orthodoxy; assumed the boldest and most uncompromising language; represented the early friends of the verse as having sustained the most flagrant injuries from the hand of the historian; and called upon the offender 'to traverse or to acknowledge, — to resist or to submit.' With regard to the composition of his work, his expression was pointed; his style, as Dr. Hey thought, was 'spirited and eloquent,'— although, in the opinion of a severer judge, too frequently gorgeous and declamatory; and his sentiments seemed to indicate a high tone of moral and religious feeling. The effect of all this was, that not being in the least scrupulous about his premises, — but plausible in his reasonings, and confident in his conclusions, — he left, I have no doubt, an impression on many minds, that uncommon abilities and acquirements had, in his own person, been conscientiously employed in the vindication of truth. His work, indeed, abounded in errors; but in errors obvious, for the most part, only to those who were tolerably versed in Scripture criticism. When, for instance, Mr. Travis asserted that 'the Latin MSS. had universally the concluding clause of the eighth verse,' and that 'the words ἐν τῇ γῇ were omitted in very few of the Greek MSS.,' how small a portion of his readers would be aware that these assertions were in direct opposition to matter of fact!

"Assertions, moreover, can seldom be verified without some trouble; and even well-informed persons, who possess the means of investigation, are too often disposed to rely upon an author's accuracy, to admit his statements, and go on to his inferences, rather than to examine the positions which are successively presented, for the purpose of ascertaining their real strength and bearings. On the whole, then, there is no reason to wonder at the temporary popularity which attended the Letters to Mr. Gibbon." *

From the extract and summary I have given, the reader may form a tolerably correct idea of the argumentation and manner of Archdeacon Travis. Never was an unfortunate author doomed to pass such an ordeal, or to endure such a flagellation as that which he was destined to undergo at the hands of Professor Porson. His Letters to Travis first appeared in the Gentleman's Magazine for 1788 and 1790. And in the last of these years, they were all republished, to the number of twelve, in an 8vo volume, entitled, "Letters to Mr. Archdeacon Travis, in answer to his Defence of the Three Heavenly Witnesses, 1 John v. 7." †

To speak of the learning, the talents, and the wit of Por-

* Crito Cantab., pp. 335 - 338.

† [Porson's Letters to Travis, now a scarce book, were reprinted in the Classical Journal, Vols. XXXVI. - XXXIX. — Ed.]

son in this place, would be a work of supererogation. He was, by universal suffrage, the most distinguished Grecian of his time, and not less celebrated for his powers of satire and invective, (unhappily too frequently exercised,) than for his knowledge of Greek literature. For the talents and acquisitions of his opponent, he entertained the most profound contempt; and for Porson to entertain an opinion, and to express it in all its strength, was a thing of course. The bearing of the dispute on any doctrine of Revelation was to him a matter of perfect indifference. How far, therefore, the doctrine of the Trinity might be affected by the discussion, he cared nothing. He approached the controversy with the reckless feelings of a giant called to crush a pygmy, and at once rushed into the thickest of the battle, regardless of everything but the accomplishment of his purpose, — the destruction of his adversary, and the expulsion from the sacred text of the long disputed passage. Justice requires that it should be said, that seldom has a more unsanctified temper been displayed in a religious discussion, than that which Porson evinced in these Letters. The defence of truth, or Christianity, is not to be desired under such circumstances. So that while our opinion coincides with that of the learned, but, alas! the unhappy Porson, we deplore that one of the ablest pieces of criticism and argument in our language should be the production of one whom no Christian can regard as an auxiliary or a friend. But it is not my business to expose the ashes of the mighty dead, farther than to deprecate the unhallowed association of impiety with a professed regard to truth and to the Scriptures.

Though Porson was not a man of serious piety, it is proper it should be stated, that he was not a Socinian. He evidently cared nothing about the matter; but his understanding was decidedly in favor of the orthodox creed on the subject of the Trinity. A friend once asked him what he thought of the evidence afforded by the New Testament in favor of the Socinian doctrines. His answer was short and decisive, — "If the New Testament is to determine the question, the Socinians are wrong." *

In these celebrated letters, Porson discusses Travis's representations of Valla's Greek MSS., which he supposed contained the disputed verse, but whose collation is shown to contain no reference to it, — his defence of the Complutensian Edition, which is proved to be unsatisfactory and futile, — his account of the MSS. used by Robert Stephens and Beza, which is exhibited as full of

"Phantoms bodiless and vain,
Empty visions of the brain," —

his representation of the MSS. supposed to be seen by the Louvain divines, and of the Dublin and Berlin copies, and his enumeration of all the Greek MSS. that omit the verse, which are proved to be not less incorrect and fallacious, — his account of the Latin Vulgate, the Syriac and Coptic, the Arabic, Ethiopic, Armenian, and Slavonic Versions, all of which are shown to be adverse to the authenticity of the witnesses, — and his representations of the Greek and Latin writers who have quoted the verse, and of those who, though they had sufficient occasion, have not quoted it.

These topics must be regarded as embracing every material point in this interesting and extended discussion. Porson fully states, and fairly meets every objection to his argument, which is most triumphantly maintained from the beginning to the end of the volume. He writes like a man who felt convinced of truth and assured of victory. He is often immeasurably severe, to which he appears to have been provoked by the ignorance and confidence of his antagonist.

* Quarterly Review, Vol. XXXIII. p. 99.

It is very singular that Travis never took notice of Porson's attack. It is impossible that he should not have known it, and equally impossible that he should not have felt it; but whether he wished his silence to be construed into contempt for the character or hatred of the talents of his adversary, cannot now be determined. Be this as it may, it is scarcely possible not to feel satisfaction in the success of Porson's efforts, or not to admire the undaunted firmness with which he meets every argument and every objection; together with his disregard of personal consequences, and his contempt for everything like chicane and subterfuge. The following, which is one of the concluding paragraphs of these letters, and which is supported by all the preceding reasonings of the volume, so fully determines the controversy, that unless it can be met and overthrown, all attempts at supporting the verse must be abortive.

"If this verse be really genuine, notwithstanding its absence from all the visible Greek MSS. except two; one of which awkwardly translates the verse from the Latin, and the other transcribes it from a printed book; notwithstanding its absence from all the Versions except the Vulgate, and even from many of the best and oldest MSS. of the Vulgate; notwithstanding the deep and dead silence of all the Greek writers down to the thirteenth and most of the Latins down to the middle of the eighth century; — if, in spite of all these objections, it be still genuine, no part of Scripture whatsoever can be proved either spurious or genuine; and Satan has been permitted, for many centuries, miraculously to banish the finest passage in the New Testament from the eyes and memories of almost all the Christian authors, translators, and transcribers." *

The general style in which Porson conducts the controversy is fairly exhibited in the following passage: —

* P. 403.

"Let us then inquire into the Greek MSS. supposed to contain the disputed verse. You, sir, reckon up seven belonging to Valla, one to Erasmus, some (you are so modest you will not say, p. 280, how many) to the Complutensian editors, sixteen to Robert Stephens, and some that the Louvain divines had seen. You afterwards make, pp. 282–285, a very pretty calculation, (for you are an excellent arithmetician,) and find that '*thirty-one* [MSS.] out of *eighty-one*, or (more than) *three* out of *eight*, or (nearly) one half of that whole number, actually did exhibit, or do exhibit, the verse, 1 John v. 7!' Inquisitive people will say, how happens it that none of these MSS. now remain, except the Dublin copy, which Wetstein is so cruel as to attribute to the sixteenth century; for concerning the Berlin MS. they will, I fear, rather choose to believe La Croze and Griesbach, than Martin and Mr. Travis. But the answer is easy. They are lost. Either they have been burned, or have been eaten by the worms, or been gnawed in pieces by the rats, or been rotted with the damps, or been destroyed by those pestilent fellows the Arians; which was very feasible; for they had only to get into their power all the MSS. of the New Testament in the world, and to mutilate or destroy those which contained *un des plus beaux passages dans l'Ecriture Sainte.* Or, if all these possibilities should fail, the Devil may play his part in the drama to great advantage. For it is a fact of which Beza *positively* assures us, that the Devil has been tampering with the text, 1 Tim. iii. 16; and that Erasmus lent him an helping hand. Beza, indeed, being a man brimful of candor, subjoins, that he believes Erasmus assisted Satan unwittingly. This, perhaps, may be some excuse for Erasmus; but what hopes of salvation are left for your Wetsteins, your Griesbachs, your Sosipaters, who have the front to persist in their damnable errors; the two first, in spite of

350 pages of Berriman; the other, in spite of 400 of Mr. Travis. After all, I rather prefer the supposition, that the Arians destroyed the said MSS., because it shows the orthodox in so superior a light; who have not, to my knowledge, at least, destroyed a single MS. that omitted their darling text, while the Arians, in less than a century and a half, suppressed thirty that contained it. Yet let us hear what may be said in their favor; not out of tenderness to them (they deserve no mercy), but merely for our own justification." *

"These letters to Archdeacon Travis," to use the words of an able critic, "form a masterpiece of literary investigation. They discover a power of discrimination to which, perhaps, a parallel can be found only in the works of Bentley. A few inaccuracies may be detected, and a few expressions brought together inconsistent with each other; but the decisions with which the volume abounds, are founded on principles which insure their stability. Mr. Porson — '*uni æquus virtuti atque ejus amicis*'— never conceals his abhorrence of disingenuous dealing in anything, but more especially in matters of religion; and he does not scruple to call such instances of it as occur to him in his inquiry, by their vulgar names." †

Sosipater, referred to in the above quotation from Porson's letters, was a writer in a work entitled "Commentaries and Essays, published by the Society for promoting the Knowledge of the Scriptures." The first volume of this work appeared without date, shortly after the publication of Travis's letters, and contains a paper by Sosipater, designated, "A Gleaning of Remarks on Mr. Travis's Attempt to revive the exploded Text of 1 John v. 7." Its contents correspond

* Letters to Travis, pp. 22 - 24.

† Quarterly Review, Vol. XXXIII. p. 99.

with the description, as they are literally gleanings, or short observations on Emlyn and Martin, and particularly the mistakes of Travis, with some extracts from Wetstein and Griesbach. He concludes by saying, "I hope I shall be excused in adding at the close of these remarks on the very extraordinary defence of this *justly* exploded text, that a more complete pattern of sophistical reasoning throughout, and of bold assertion without proof, I never met with, and that if my voice could extend itself to Mr. Gibbon, in his distant abode on the lake *Leman;* to whom, it may be presumed, a series of letters addressed to him have been communicated; I would entrêat that gentleman not to judge of his opponents, and of all the defenders of Christianity, by this its present champion and advocate, Mr. Travis."

The work in which this paper appeared extended only to two volumes. I believe Dr. Disney was the conductor of it; and the writers were mostly, if not entirely, Unitarians. Sosipater was the late Theophilus Lindsey, who wrote a considerable number of papers under that signature.

One of the leading points in this discussion relates to the readings of the Greek MSS. employed by Robert Stephens, in the construction of the text of his celebrated edition of the New Testament, and to the placing of the crotchet referred to by Mr. Gibbon. From the complicated nature of this controversy, and the numerous minute points which it involves, it is very difficult to give an abridged view of this part of the argument. It appears that of the sixteen codices, including the Complutensian, used by Stephens, only seven contained the Catholic Epistles; consequently no more could be employed in his collation of the disputed verse. In his text he shows the number of words omitted in any of his MSS., by prefixing an obelus † before the first word, and a little crotchet ), or semicircle, after the last word. In the disputed text, he places his obelus and crotchet as under: † ἐν τῷ οὐρανῷ) ὁ πατὴρ, ὁ λόγος, κ.τ.λ. By which he appears to intimate that not the whole verse, but only the words ἐν τῷ οὐρανῷ were omitted in his seven MSS. Whether the placing of the crotchet in this position, instead of the end of the verse, was by design, or a mistake of Stephens, or his compositor, it is impossible now to ascertain. The latter is by far the more probable supposition.

The friends of the disputed passage, among whom must be ranked, in particular, Mr. Travis, consider it as most evident, that the MSS. employed by Stephens contained the passage, and every possible effort has been made to maintain this ground. It is clear, however, that if the Stephenic MSS. remain, and can be identified, they must furnish the most conclusive proof of the actual reading. And as Stephens refers to all the seven by one indication, should even one of the seven be found and that not contain the passage, it would be conclusive against the whole. It happens that no Greek MS., at present known, omits only the three words to which the notation of the Stephenic text is limited. Four of the seven MSS. employed by Stephens on the Catholic Epistles were borrowed from the Royal Library at Paris, and returned after being used. It was found by Simon, more than a hundred years ago, that not a single MS. in the Royal Library at Paris contained the disputed text. And as four of Stephens's seven were included in those MSS., though which four had not been ascertained, little doubt could be entertained of Stephens's mistake.

Le Long, in 1720, undertook to ascertain the four very MSS. belonging to the Royal Library used by Stephens. He succeeded in identifying them; and found they omitted the whole verse. From this period Stephens's semicircle was abandoned to its fate, till Archdeacon Travis took a journey to Paris, in 1791, with a view to recollate the MSS. on which Le Long had fixed, as the seven which were used by Stephens. The effect of his examination was a full confidence on his part that Le Long had been mistaken in the MSS., that the crotchet stands in the proper place in the text of Stephens, and "that the calumniated memory of Stephens would be redeemed to its ancient honors." But all this is no better than idle vaunting, for Travis only proved himself to be totally unfit for the task of examining and collating Greek MSS., as no doubt can be entertained of the identity of the MSS. in question.

Four of the seven MSS. used by Stephens, containing the Catholic Epistles, and referred to by the mistaken placing of his crotchet, as if they read the disputed verse, being thus ascertained, and found not to contain it; during the interval of 1791 and 1794, when Travis's last edition of his letters appeared, Mr., now Dr. Marsh, Bishop of Peterborough, thought he discovered another of those MSS. in the Library of the University of Cambridge. And in the year 1793, in a note to the second volume of his Translation of Michaelis's Introduction to the New Testament, he intimated this discovery. This MS. had once belonged to Vatablus, the friend of Stephens, and perfectly corresponds with the Codex Stephani ιγ. This MS. also omits the whole of the disputed verse; and thus five of Stephens's seven MSS., containing the Catholic Epistles, have been discovered, and are found to want the passage. The two other MSS. have not yet, I believe, been found, but the question, as to all the MSS., must be regarded as settled.

This note of Dr. Marsh, Travis attacked in the last edition of his Letters to Gibbon. The following is the passage:—

"In addition to these adversaries, the learned translator

of Michaelis has lately informed the world, that the MS. distinguished by the letters ιγ by R. Stephens, is now in the Library of the University of Cambridge, is there marked Kk. 6. 4, and that it contains the Epistle of St. John, but not the verse, 1 John v. 7. His argument on this subject may be reduced to the following heads.

"1. The readings which R. Stephens has produced from the MS. ιγ alone, throughout the Catholic Epistles, amount to twenty.

"2. These singular readings are all found 'without any exception, and without the least variation' in his MS. Kk.

"3. Several of these singular readings have been discovered in no MS. whatever since the days of R. Stephens.

"4. This extraordinary coincidence, united with the circumstance that the MS. Kk has the name of a contemporary, and a friend of R. Stephens in it, affords the strongest proof that the MS. now in question, and the MS. ιγ of R. Stephens, are one and the same book; and therefore,

"5. The semicircle of R. Stephens is misplaced.

"The observations on this argument, founded on an examination of the Catholic Epistles in this MS. Kk, shall follow the order in which the several parts of that argument are here arranged.

"1. On referring to the margin of R. Stephens, it will appear that he has quoted his MS. ιγ *solely*, not merely in twenty, but in twenty-five places.

"2. One of these singular readings, which is *not found* in the MS. Kk, is in James v. 7, in which passage this copy reads εως λαβη καρπον πρωιμον και οψιμον. But the MS. ιγ reads the passage thus, ιγ εως αν λαβη πρωιμον και οψιμον, without καρπον or any other substantive. This may, perhaps, be one of those five passages which Mr. Marsh did not reckon. It renders his whole argument ineffective, although the other twenty-four singular readings should be (as on examination they appear to be) in the MS. Kk.

"3. As to the assertion that several of these singular readings have been discovered in no MS. whatever since the days of R. Stephens, it will appear, on consulting the various readings collected by Mill, Wetstein, and Griesbach, that the case stands thus, or nearly thus. Of the twenty-four singular readings in which the MS. ιγ and Kk agree, twelve have been discovered in other Greek MSS., six more have been found in some of the oldest versions, and one more in Cyril of Alexandria; so that there are only five singular readings which have not yet been found any where except in the MSS. Kk and ιγ.

"4. Mr. Marsh infers from this extraordinary coincidence, (a coincidence of twelve readings,) and from the word Vatablus being written in the MS. Kk, that it must be the MS. ιγ of R. Stephens. It will instantly appear how insignificant the latter circumstance is. And with regard to the former, if it be a just inference that two MSS. are the same because they agree in a certain number of passages, where they deviate from all other copies; it is surely reasonable to conclude, that if one of two given MSS. shall disagree, not only with the other, but also with the rest of the MSS. which have hitherto been collated, in a far greater number of passages, they must be two different MSS.

"In the MS. Kk, there are in all 135 deviations from the text of R. Stephens, each of them not less important than those which he has produced from his MS. ιγ. In his margin the MS. ιγ is quoted only 60 times. There are in the MS. Kk, therefore, 75 more various readings than R. Stephens has produced from the MS. ιγ.

"Among the 135 readings, just mentioned, there are 42 which are not to be met with, either in the margin of R.

Stephens, or in the various readings of Mill, of Wetstein, or of Griesbach; that is, there are 42 passages wherein the MS. Kk differs, not only from the MS. ιγ, (as the fair presumption is,) but from every other known MS. But there are twelve places alone in which the MS. ιγ is known to agree with the MS. Kk, and to differ from every other copy. From all which facts and circumstances taken together, it appears most probable that the copies now in question are two different MSS. And therefore that

"5. Mr. Marsh's argument does *not* shew that the semicircle of R. Stephens is misplaced.

"It will not be too strong an observation to remark, that such accusations tarnish not his well-earned honors. They prove nothing — but the precipitancy of his accusers." *

It was in defence of his note, therefore, and in farther support of his own views, and those of Michaelis,† on 1 John v. 7, that this learned writer published at Leipsic, where he was then residing, the following able volume; "Letters to Mr. Archdeacon Travis, in Vindication of one of the Translator's Notes to Michaelis's Introduction, and in confirmation of the opinion that a Greek MS. now preserved in the Public Library of the University of Cambridge, is one of the seven which are quoted by R. Stephens, at 1 John v. 7. With an Appendix, containing a Review of Mr. Travis's Collation of the Greek MSS. which he examined in Paris; an Extract from Mr. Pappelbaum's Treatise on the Berlin MS.; and

* Travis's Letters, pp. 410–414.

† Mr. Butler, by mistake, represents Michaelis as at first an advocate for the disputed verse, and refers to a book, by him, on that side of the question, and to another also in opposition to it. — Horæ Biblicæ, Vol. I. p. 379. What he affirms of Michaelis, belongs to Semler, who changed his views, and wrote both the works which Mr. Butler ascribes to Michaelis.— See Marsh's Michaelis, Vol. VI. p. 413.

an Essay on the Origin and Object of the Velesian Readings." 8vo. 1795.

These letters, seven in number, with the appendices, supplied everything that was wanting to complete the discomfiture and disgrace of the unfortunate Archdeacon. They deprive him not only of every shadow of argument, but clearly prove that he resorted to artifice to support the cause he had rashly undertaken to defend. It is impossible to convey an idea of the labor, research, and learning, which this admirable volume displays. It is worth being consulted as an exercise of the understanding, and of being referred to as a specimen of the most admirably sustained argumentation. The main positions are established by a superfluity of proof, so that the reader has no option but to adopt the conclusion respecting the identity of the MSS., the misplacing of the crotchet, and consequently that none of the MSS. used by Stephens really contained this passage. On every point, indeed, involved in this discussion, much curious and accurate information is communicated, so that the reader will find it one of the most valuable works in the whole range of biblical criticism. One of the most curious applications of mathematical science to moral evidence is contained in this work. By the application of a mathematical theorem, in the fourth letter, to the documents produced in the second and fifth letters, the learned writer endeavors to show that the probability in favor of the MS. Kk. 6. 4, in the University of Cambridge, being one of the MSS. collated by Stephens, is, to the probability of the contrary, as two nonillions to unity. This he conceives, if the calculation be correct, every one will consider as amounting to a moral certainty.

Various opinions may be entertained respecting the propriety of applying mathematical science to such subjects; and also respecting the perfect accuracy of the algebraic formula on which he reasons; but only one opinion can exist respecting the point to which it is applied. Dr. Marsh's account of the steps by which he was led to the result at which he finally arrived, is singularly interesting, and though long, as it affords a beautiful specimen of critical caution and acumen, and as the volume is now scarcely to be procured at any price, the reader, I am sure, will be pleased to be furnished with it.

"In the beginning of the year 1793, while I was printing my Notes to the second volume of Michaelis's Introduction, I examined the manuscripts of the Greek Testament, preserved in the University Library, of which I had made a catalogue in the preceding summer. My attention was particularly engaged by that which was marked Kk. 6. 4.: a manuscript containing the Acts of the Apostles, with the Catholic Epistles, and those of St. Paul. I found, on examination, that it bore the appearance of a very respectable antiquity, that its readings were in numerous examples different from the common printed text, where the deviations were supported by very few other authorities, and I was surprised that so remarkable a manuscript should, as I at that time supposed, have remained uncollated. Considering, however, that manuscripts, after the death of their proprietors, are frequently transferred to different libraries, and sometimes even to distant countries, I thought it not improbable that this manuscript, though never quoted as a Codex Cantabrigiensis, might have been collated and quoted by a different name before it was purchased for the University Library, in the same manner as the Codex Augiensis, now in Trinity College, was in the beginning of this century collated by Wetstein, in the library of Mr. Mieg at Heidelberg. And that the very same thing had really happened to the MS. Kk. 6. 4., I was led to conclude by the following circumstances. In the first place

I observed the name of Vatablus (who was Hebrew Professor in the University of Paris, and died about the middle of the sixteenth century) written on the inside of the cover, at the beginning of the manuscript, in a place where the proprietors of books very frequently write their names. The same name I saw likewise at the end of the manuscript, and observed that in both places the name was written in the middle of the page, and in the same hand. I perceived likewise the name of Hautin written at the beginning of the manuscript, in the same page with the name of Vatablus, but in a different hand, and in a different part of the page, namely, in one of the upper corners, which is likewise a place where the proprietors of books very frequently write their names. I concluded therefore that the manuscript had been formerly in France, and successively the property of Vatablus and Hautin. I paid, however, little attention to the name of Hautin: it was that of Vatablus which led me to further inquiries, and first excited the suspicion that this manuscript might have been one of those which were used by R. Stephens for his editions of the Greek Testament, printed in 1546, 1549, and 1550, because Vatablus was one of Robert Stephens's intimate friends, and was likewise connected with him in his literary pursuits. Under these circumstances I thought it impossible that an ancient and valuable manuscript, in the possession of Vatablus, could have been unknown to Stephens: and, as he expressly declares in the preface to his edition of 1550, that he procured six manuscripts from various quarters, in addition to the eight borrowed from the Royal Library (which with the Complutensian edition and the manuscript collated in Italy make up the sixteen), it appeared to me at least probable, that the Codex Vatabli was one of the six. Further, this probability was greatly increased by the strong expression which Stephens has used in speaking of these six manuscripts, for he says that they were 'ea, quæ undique corrogare licuit.' The word 'undique' plainly denotes that he collected from various quarters; and the addition of 'licuit' is a proof that he collected at least such as he thought worthy of notice, where he was able to procure them.

"Having thus considered the probability, that the Codex Vatabli had been used by Stephens, derived from external evidence, I proceeded to inquire what internal evidence might be obtained in its favor. For this purpose, it was necessary to fix upon some one of Stephens's manuscripts, and compare the readings which Stephens had quoted from it, with the readings of the Codex Vatabli: and I was led to fix on one of the two marked ια and ιγ, in the following manner. I considered that if the Codex Vatabli had been used by Stephens, it must be one of the six 'quæ undique corrogare licuit'; for, independently of the arguments already adduced to show that it probably was one of those six, it could neither be the Codex α nor β, for reasons which it would be superfluous to mention: neither could it be one of the eight manuscripts marked by Stephens, γ, δ, ε, ϛ, ζ, η, ι, ιε, for these eight, as he himself declares, were borrowed from the Royal Library. If used at all, therefore, it could be only one of the six which Stephens has noted by θ, ια, ιβ, ιγ, ιδ, ιϛ. But it could neither be the θ, nor the ιβ, nor the ιδ; for the two first of these have been discovered by Wetstein to be the same as the Codex Coislinianus 200, and the Codex Regius 83; and the third has been found by Griesbach to be the Codex Victorinus 774. The number therefore of the undiscovered Codices Stephanici were reduced to the three marked ια, ιγ, ιϛ: but the Codex ιϛ is quoted by Stephens above fifty times in the Apocalypse, a book which is not contained in the Codex Vatabli. There remained therefore for trial only the ια and the ιγ, both of which, as appears from the quotations in Stephens's margin, contained the very same books as the Codex Vatabli, namely, the Acts of the Apostles, the Catholic Epistles, and those of St. Paul.

"Having discovered so far, that one of these two manuscripts *might* be the Codex Vatabli, I resolved further to examine whether either of them actually *were*. To this end I copied from Stephens's margin, throughout the Catholic Epistles, (which I thought a sufficient portion for determining the question, without going also through the Acts of the Apostles, and the Epistles of St. Paul,) all the singular readings of the two MSS. ια and ιγ, or, in other words, such as Stephens had quoted from each of these manuscripts solely. Those of the former amounted to twenty, those of the latter to twenty-five. Having formed in this manner, from Stephens's margin, two separate catalogues of the characteristic readings of these two manuscripts, I went into the Public Library to compare them with the Codex Vatabli: and in case I found that this manuscript contained the whole series of characteristic readings, either of the Codex ια, or of the Codex ιγ, — all proper allowances being made for typographical errors, from which Stephens's margin is by no means free, — I thought I should be justified in concluding that I had discovered one of the manuscripts of Robert Stephens, which had been buried in oblivion since the middle of the sixteenth century. The first trial which I made, was with the characteristic readings of the Codex ια: but I soon perceived that this could not be the manuscript, for not one of its characteristic readings, as far as I compared, was to be found in the Codex Vatabli. My last resource therefore was the Codex ιγ, and if the internal evidence had there likewise been as unfavorable as to the Codex ια, I must have abandoned the opinion that the Codex Vatabli had been used by

Stephens, notwithstanding the external evidence in its favor. But to my great surprise, and I acknowledge to my great satisfaction, I found in the Codex Vatabli *all* the singular readings of the Codex ιγ, throughout the Catholic Epistles; which is really more than I should have expected, even had I known for certain before I made the comparison, that the Codex Vatabli was the very manuscript which Stephens denoted by the mark ιγ, since among twenty-five readings in Stephens's margin, taken any where at a venture, we may in general expect to find at least one error, either of the collator, or of the printer. This extraordinary coincidence, therefore, between the characteristic readings of the Codex ιγ and those of the Codex Vatabli, united with the external evidence derived from the manuscript's having been the property of one of Stephens's intimate friends, afforded, as I thought, and as I still think, a very satisfactory proof of their identity. Further, upon consulting the editions of Mill, Wetstein, and Griesbach, I found, 1st, that of the twenty-five singular readings of the Codex ιγ, no manuscript at present known, beside the Codex Vatabli, contains even a sixth part; 2dly, that if we except the Codex Alexandrinus, which contains four of them, and four only, there is no single manuscript at present known which contains any two of them; and 3dly, that all the manuscripts put together, which have been collated by Mill, Wetstein, and Griesbach (to whom, as I have since learnt, may be added Matthäi and Alter), contain only two fifths of them. Whether under these circumstances I rightly concluded, that if any *one* manuscript was found to contain them *all*, it could be no other than the very manuscript from which they had been taken, or whether the inference was made with that 'precipitancy' of which you have thought proper to accuse me, I leave to be determined by those who are competent judges." *

* Marsh's Letters, pp. 3 – 9.

The following passage will show his views and feelings respecting the moral and intellectual qualities of his antagonist.

"Here I would willingly close this subject; but as you, yourself, are so extremely liberal of censure, even in cases where you ought rather to applaud, you must not expect to escape, where censure is justly due. The expression, 'shameful debility,' which you apply to Le Long, Wetstein, and Griesbach, might be retorted, not four but fourscore fold upon yourself; for of an hundred examples which you have produced, pp. 220 – 241, and which have been the subject of the preceding inquiry, there are more than seventy which are either false, or prove nothing, or prove against yourself. When I find you arguing from Stephens's silence, and concluding that his MSS. agreed with his text, wherever he has not specified the contrary, or when I see you gravely copying Stephens's own words, and producing them as various readings of a Greek MS., I have no other sensation than that of pity for a man, who has imprudently engaged in sacred criticism, without possessing the necessary qualifications. But when I meet with assertions that cannot be ascribed to want of knowledge; when I find you quoting Stephens for evidence which he has not given, and suppressing that which he really has, and consider that there are instances of the former kind, in which you could hardly have been taken by surprise, and examples of the latter, in which you neither could have been ignorant of what Stephens had quoted, nor of the impossibility of concealing that quotation, without leading your readers into error, it is really difficult to avoid giving way to the feelings of a just indignation." *

This volume may be considered as concluding the direct controversy occasioned by Gibbon's attack. Travis never returned to the charge. He died about this time, not without

* Pp. 238 – 240.

a suspicion that the controversy severely affected his health, and contributed to shorten his days.

In 1801, Dr. Marsh published the second part of the translation of Michaelis's Introduction. The last volume of this work contains a Dissertation of that learned German on the passage in question; in which, among other things, he gives a short account of what had been published in Germany, in defence of the passage, subsequently to 1750, the year in which the first edition of his Introduction appeared, and in which he had expressed his opinion that the passage was spurious.

"The first is a thesis written for a public disputation by Dr. Semler, at Halle, in 1751, entitled, 'Vindiciæ plurium præcipuarum lectionum codicis Græci Novi Testamenti, adversus Whistonum, atque ab eo latas leges criticas.' This tract eminently distinguishes itself from the rest by its profound learning, and great moderation. It would be superfluous to make any reply to it at present, because the learned author himself, who soon after altered his opinion, not only confuted all the arguments which had been used in favor of 1 John v. 7, but wrote the most important work which we have on this subject.*

"The next defence of 1 John v. 7 was written by Mr. J. E. Wagner, in 1752, and entitled 'Integritas commatis septimi capitis quinti primæ Joannis epistolæ ab impugnationibus novatoris cujusdam denuo vindicata.' This treatise was directed particularly against me, whom the author meant by

* [The work referred to bears the following title: — "Historische und kritische Sammlungen über die so genannten Beweisstellen in der Dogmatik. Erstes Stück. Über 1 Joh. 5, 7." I. e. Historical and Critical Collections relating to the so-called Proof-texts in Dogmatic Theology. Part I. On 1 John v. 7. Halle und Helmstädt, 1764, 8vo. pp. 20, 429, besides Index.— Part II., which I have not seen, appeared in 1768. — Ed.]

his '*novator quidam.*' But with such an adversary as Mr. Wagner I never could persuade myself to enter into any controversy.

"After a lapse of above thirty years, the learned Knittel undertook another defence of the disputed passage in his 'New Criticisms on 1 John v. 7,' printed at Brunswick, in 1785. This is a valuable work, and much useful information may be derived from it; but in the proof of the principal point the author has totally failed.

"In the same year, Mr. Travis published in London his 'Letters to Gibbon'; and in the year following, Mr. Stresow printed at Hamburgh his 'Open Avowal of the Doctrine of the Trinity, as delivered in 1 John v. 7.' But both of these publications betrayed the utmost partiality and ignorance."*

The greatest part of Michaelis's dissertation is occupied in combating the ground on which Bengel had rested the defence of the text, which is done in a very masterly and convincing manner. The sixth section is occupied with Michaelis's view of the manner in which the passage was introduced into the Latin copies, from which little doubt can be entertained it was afterwards translated into Greek, and thus obtained possession, first of one Greek MS., and then of the Complutensian Edition. As the section is short, I shall give it entire.

"When it has been proved, by satisfactory evidence, that a passage is spurious, it is wholly unnecessary to show at what time or in what manner the passage was first introduced. There are many readings in our common printed text, which, at present, are universally allowed to be false, though we cannot ascertain by what copyist they were first written, or what particular cause has given them birth. In such cases we must be satisfied with probable conjecture; for his

* Marsh's Michaelis, Vol. VI. pp. 413, 414.

torical evidence is seldom to be expected, since interpolations are in general clandestine facts, and are very rarely recorded. But since the advocates of 1 John v. 7 contend that this passage would not have been contained in the Latin version unless it had been contained likewise in the Greek, I will endeavor to show in what manner it was first introduced into the Latin version.

"The simple fact, that it had its origin in the Latin, is indisputable, since it is contained in no ancient Greek manuscript, and in no other version. And the cause which gave it birth was probably the following: It appears from the third section of this chapter, that the African fathers interpreted 1 John v. 8 mystically, and considered 'the spirit, the water, and the blood,' as denoting the Father, the Son, and the Holy Ghost. Further it must be remarked, that the African fathers were the first who discovered 1 John v. 7 in the Latin version. The combination of these two facts leads to the following probable conclusion; that the spiritual interpretation of 1 John v. 8 was written in the margin of one or more Latin manuscripts, and that in order to distinguish the terrestrial from the celestial meaning, the words 'in terra' were added as a marginal gloss, in reference to 'testimonium dant' in the eighth verse, by which means both the literal and the spiritual meaning were rendered perfect. According to this representation the text and the margin stood thus:—

| Margin | Text |
|---|---|
| * in terra.<br><br>Et tres sunt, qui testimonium dant in cœlo, Pater, Verbum, et Spiritus Sanctus: et hi tres unum sunt. | "Quoniam tres sunt, qui testimonium dant,* spiritus, et aqua, et sanguis: et hi tres unum sunt." |

When a copy of this kind fell into the hands of ignorant transcribers, who were making new transcripts of the Latin Bible, they imagined that what was written in the margin was a part of the text, which had been omitted by mistake consequently they inserted it in the text of the manuscript which they themselves were writing. But some of them inserted the marginal reading before the text, of which it was the interpretation, others after it; and this is the reason why the controverted passage has no fixed place in the Latin manuscripts, — the heavenly witnesses sometimes preceding, sometimes following the earthly witnesses.

"In this manner the passage having gained admittance into one or more Latin manuscripts written in Africa, it had the undeserved good fortune to be quoted in the Confession of Faith presented at the end of the fifth century by the African bishops to Huneric, king of the Vandals. And as these bishops became martyrs, and were said even to have performed a miracle, the passage, in consequence of its having been quoted in their Confession, not only acquired celebrity, but was stamped with authority. Hence other Latin transcribers, especially they who lived in Africa, were induced to follow the example of those who transferred the passage from the margin to the text. And, as the Carthaginian and Roman churches were closely allied, this example soon spread itself to the transcribers who lived in Italy. It must be observed, however, that the example was not imitated universally; for Facundus, who lived in the sixth century, did not find the passage in his manuscript of the Latin version. This appears from the circumstance that he proves the doctrine of the Trinity by a mystical interpretation of the eighth verse; which he certainly would not have done if the seventh verse had been contained in his manuscript, because in this verse the doctrine which he intended to prove is literally and directly asserted. After the sixth century the whole Latin Church was involved in ignorance and barbarism; all critical inquiries were at an end; and both spurious and genuine passages were received without distinction. In the Middle-Ages, therefore, 1 John v. 7 was generally considered throughout the West of Europe as a part of St. John's first Epistle, without any further questions being asked about it." *

Such is the decided opinion of one of the most learned, candid, and ingenious critics which Germany ever produced, of the spuriousness of this passage, and of the method in which it crept into the text. His explanation is not founded on mere conjecture or hypothesis, but on circumstances belonging to the state of the Latin MSS. which strongly support the view which he has given.

In 1807, Dr. Adam Clarke published his useful work, "The Succession of Sacred Literature"; † to which he prefixes two fac-similes of the disputed passage; one taken from the Complutensian Edition of the New Testament, and the other from the Codex Montfortii in Trinity College, Dublin. In treating on the first Epistle of John, he makes some judicious observations on the text of the three witnesses, in order to illustrate his plates. After stating his opinion of the age of the Codex Montfortianus, which has been already given, he proceeds as follows: —

"Though a conscientious advocate for the *sacred doctrine* contained in the disputed text, and which I think expressly enough revealed in several other parts of the sacred writings, yet I must own the passage in question stands on a most dubious foundation. All the Greek manuscripts (the Codex Montfortii alone excepted) omit the passage: so do *all* the *ancient versions*, the *Vulgate* excepted: but in many of the ancient MSS. even of this version it is wanting. There is one in the British Museum, of the tenth or eleventh century, where it is added by a more recent hand in the margin: for

* Pp. 434-437.

† [A second edition, enlarged, was published in 1831. — ED.]

it is wanting also in the text. It is also *variously written* in those manuscripts which retain it. This will appear more plainly by comparing the following extracts, taken from four manuscripts of the Vulgate in my own possession: — .

"1. Quoniam tres sunt qui testimonium dant in cœlo Pater, Verbum et Spiritus Sanctus et hii tres unum sunt. Et tres sunt qui testimonium dant in terra, Spiritus, Sanguis et Aqua.

"2. Quoniam tres sunt qui testimonium dant in terra, Spiritus, Aqua et Sanguis, et tres unum sunt. Et tres sunt qui testimonium dant in cœlo Pater Verbum et Spiritus Sanctus, et hii tres unum sunt.

"3. Quoniam tres sunt qui testimonium dant in cœlo, Pater, et Filius et Spiritus Sanctus, et hii tres unum sunt. Et tres sunt qui testimonium dant in terra, Spiritus, Aqua et Sanguis.

"4. Quoniam tres sunt qui testimonium dant in terra, spiritus, aqua et sanguis; et hii tres unum sunt. Et tres sunt qui testimonium dant in Cælo, Pater et Filius et Spiritus Sanctus, et hii tres unum sunt.

"5. Quoniam tres sunt qui Testimonium dant in terra Spiritus, Aqua et Sanguis, et tres sunt qui testimonium perhibent in Cœlo Pater, Verbum, et Spiritus Sanctus et hi tres unum sunt.

"This last I took from an ancient manuscript in Marsh's Library, St. Patrick's, Dublin.

"In the Bible printed by Fradin and Pinard, Paris, 1497, fol., the text is the same with No. 2, only instead of *testimonium dant*, it reads *dant testimonium*.

"The reader will observe, that in No. 2, 4, and 5, the *eighth* verse is put *before* the *seventh*, and that 3 and 4 have *filius* instead of *verbum*. But both these readings are united in an ancient English manuscript of my own, which contains the Bible from the beginning of Proverbs to the end of the New Testament, written on thick strong vellum, and evidently prior to the time of Wicliff.

"For three ben that geven witnessing in heven the Fadir, the Word or Sone and the Hooly Goost, and these three ben oon. And three ben that geven witnessing in erthe, the Spirit, Water, and Blood, and these three ben oon.

"As many suppose the Complutensian editors must have had a manuscript or manuscripts which contained this disputed passage, I judge it necessary to add the *note* which they subjoin at the bottom of the page, by which (though nothing is clearly expressed) it appears they either had such a manuscript, or *wished to have it thought they had such.* However, the note is curious, and shows us how this disputed passage was read in the most approved manuscripts of the Vulgate extant in the thirteenth century, when St. Thomas Aquinas wrote, from whom this note is taken.

"The following is the whole note *literatim:* —

"'Sanctus Thomas in expositione secunde Decretalis de suma Trinitate et fide catholica tractans istum passum contra Abbatem Joachim ut tres sunt qui testimonium dant in celo. Pater: Verbum: et Spiritus Sanctus: dicit ad litteram verba sequentia. Et ad insinuandam unitatem trium personarum subditur, Et hii tres unum sunt. Quodquidem dicitur propter essentie unitatem. Sed hoc Joachim perverse trahere volens ad unitatem charitatis et consensus inducebat consequentem auctoritatem. Nam subditur ibidem: Et tres sunt qui testimonium dant in terra. s. Spiritus: Aqua: et Sanguis. Et in quibusdam libris additur: Et hii tres unum sunt. Sed hoc in veris exemplaribus non habetur: sed dicitur esse appositum ab hereticis Arrianis ad pervertendum intellectum sanum auctoritatis premisse de unitate essentie trium personarum. Hec beatus Thomas ubi supra.' *

* [That is: — " Saint Thomas, in his exposition of the second Decretal concerning the Most High Trinity and the Catholic faith, treating of this passage, 'There are three that bear witness in heaven, the Father, the Word, and the Holy Spirit,' in opposition to the Abbot Joachim, uses pre-

"If the Complutensian editors *translated* the passage into Greek from the *Vulgate*, it is strange they made no mention of it in this place, where they had so fair an opportunity, while speaking so very pointedly on the doctrine in question, and forming a note for the occasion, which is indeed the only theological note in the whole volume. It is again worthy of note, that, when these editors found an important various reading in any of their Greek manuscripts, they noted it in the margin: an example occurs 1 Cor. xvi. 51.—Why was it then that they took no notice of so important an *omission* as the text of the three witnesses, if they really had no manuscript in which it was contained? Did they intend to *deceive* the reader, and could they possibly imagine that the knavery should never be detected? If they designed to deceive, they took the most effectual way to conceal the fraud, as it is probable they destroyed the manuscripts from which they printed their text; for the story of their being sold in 1749 to a *rocket-maker*, (see Michaelis, Vol. II. p. 440,) is every way so exceptionable and unlike the truth, that I really wonder there should be found any person who would seriously give it credit. It is more likely the manuscripts were destroyed at first, or that they are still *kept secret*, to prevent the forgery (if it be one) of the text of the three witnesses from being detected; or the librarian already mentioned may have converted them to *his own use*. If they were not destroyed by

cisely the following language:—'And to teach the unity of the three persons it is subjoined, *And these three are one;* which is said on account of their unity of essence. But Joachim, wishing perversely to refer this to a unity of affection and agreement, alleged the text that follows it. For it is immediately subjoined, *And there are three that bear witness on earth,* namely, *the Spirit, the water, and the blood.* And in some books it is added, *And these three are one.* But this is not contained in the true copies, but is said to have been added by the Arian heretics to prevent the text that precedes from being correctly understood as relating to the unity of essence of the three persons.'—Thus the blessed Thomas, as above referred to."—ED.]

the Complutensian editors, I should not be surprised if the same manuscripts should come to light in some other part of the world, if not in the Alcala library itself." *

It is worthy of notice in this part of this important controversy, that Dr. Clarke's suspicion of the story of the rocket-maker, who is alleged to have purchased the MSS. from which the Complutensian edition was formed, and who was of course supposed to have exploded them long ago, turns out to be well founded; and his anticipation that they might one day be discovered has at length been realized. I copy the following passage from a pamphlet recently published by Dr. Smith.

"Mr. T. quotes the Bishop of Peterborough's third edition of his translation of Michaelis, to show that the learned Bishop has changed his opinion, and now believes the manuscripts from which the Complutensian text was taken to have been more ancient and valuable than, agreeably to the general opinion, he had before supposed. This is, however, a matter which does not at all affect our argument. Undoubtedly, for reasons of critical curiosity and satisfaction, we should be gratified by knowing the character and history of the Alcala manuscripts; yet there is the highest moral certainty that this knowledge would do nothing more than confirm what is already well enough known. In fact, the matter is established: for there is good reason to believe that the learned Germans, Moldenhauer and Tychsen, were the subjects of an imposition practised upon them by some people in the Spanish University, who were not disposed to permit their manuscript treasures to be scrutinized by Protestants. A gentleman with whom I have the honor of acquaintance, well known as a friend of rational freedom and a sufferer in

* Pp. 92-97.

its cause, and whose extraordinary talents as a linguist and a poet have eminently enriched our literature, John Bowring, Esq., has spent much time in Spain, and was the intimate friend of the most enlightened, learned, and patriotic men in that country during its enjoyment of the blessing (of which it has been so basely and cruelly robbed!) of a constitutional government. He had the opportunity of carefully examining the manuscripts at Alcala; he has published reasons amounting to a demonstration that *no sale or destruction of manuscripts ever took place;* by his personal examination he found THE SAME Scripture manuscripts which had been described as being in the library, by Alvaro Gomez, who died in 1580; and he adds, 'That the manuscripts referred to are *modern* and *valueless* there can be no longer any question.' To Mr. Bowring I am also indebted for the information (which, had it been known to Michaelis, or to his learned translator, would have been to them most welcome intelligence, and would have saved them a world of trouble) that Gomez, in his *Life of Cardinal Ximenes,* states that '*Leo X. lent to Ximenes those* [Greek manuscripts which] *he required from the Vatican;* which were returned as soon as the Polyglot was completed.' " *

According to this statement, unless some MSS. in the Vatican, yet unexamined, shall be found to contain the testimony of the heavenly witnesses, which is in the highest degree improbable, it must be admitted that the Complutensian editors translated the passage into Greek from the Latin Vulgate; and thus one of the main arguments on which its authenticity has been erected will be entirely overthrown.

The various readings of the Latin MSS. given by Dr. Clarke, and which are only a specimen of the diversity that obtains in this passage in the MSS. of the Vulgate, create a

* Smith's Rejoinder to Taylor, 1829, pp. 48, 49.

strong suspicion that there is something radically unsound in the authority of the verse. The unique theological note also which Dr. Clarke gives from the Complutensian, in the very ambiguity which pervades it, savors strongly of management. It was felt desirable to support the authority of the Vulgate, and yet it was deemed imprudent to assert that the passage was found in the Greek MSS. Had the evidence been satisfactory, it would have been more distinctly indicated.

In the same year in which Dr. Clarke's work was published, a series of papers on the disputed passage, by an acute and well-informed writer,* appeared in the Christian Observer. These papers, had they been printed separately, which they deserved to be, would have made a considerable pamphlet. They give a very lucid view of the principal points of evidence for and against the authenticity of the passage; with the author's own observations on some of the writers on both sides. He discusses very ably the state of the first editions of the Greek Testament, the testimony of the Greek MSS., that of the ancient fathers [versions], and the Greek and Latin fathers, all of which he shows to be unfavorable to the authority of the passage. His mode of accounting for the mistake, or supposed mistake, of Stephens, in placing the crotchet, to which we have already referred, seems very satisfactory.

"The arguments that have been urged in this and the foregoing chapter concerning Stephens's MSS. may be thus briefly stated.

"First. Neither the MSS. of the Complutensian editors, nor those of Erasmus, nor any of the 150 which now exist, except two, both of modern date, contain 1 John v. 7. Hence

* [The Rev. Joseph Jowett, LL. D., Professor of Civil Law in the University of Cambridge. See Horne's Introduction, Vol. IV. p. 386, 10th edit. — Ed.]

it seems highly improbable that it should be found in all Stephens's MSS., collected as they were from various quarters.

"Secondly. He returned to the Royal Library the MSS. which he had borrowed from it. Yet Simon, after a diligent search in that library, did not discover that verse in a single MS.

"Thirdly. Two MSS. of the Epistles of St. John, which have been compared with the collations of Stephens's θ and ιγ, from an extraordinary coincidence of readings, are inferred to be the very MSS. employed by that editor. If this inference be allowed, the conclusion is inevitable that his θ and ιγ had not the seventh verse, because it is in neither of the MSS. with which they have been compared.

"These arguments amount to a very high degree of presumptive evidence; but great probabilities may be overcome by testimony. Let us then attend to the testimony produced upon this occasion.

"First. Robert Stephens, in his Latin Testament, 1545, says that some Greek copies read thus: Tres sunt qui testimonium dant Pater, &c., omitting *in cœlo.*

"Secondly. In his Greek Testament of 1550, he includes ἐν τῷ οὐρανῷ between marks, and, in the margin, names seven MSS., in which he says these words are wanting.

"Thirdly. In 1556 he printed Beza's Latin Testament, where, in a note on 1 John v. 7, are the following words: 'Legimus et nos in nonnullis Roberti nostri veteribus libris,' and on the words *in cœlo*, 'Hoc deerat in 7 vetustis codicibus.' Now if Stephens had no such reading in his MSS., how can these repeated assertions be accounted for? We cannot suppose that he intended to deceive, where, as Mr Porson observes, he has furnished every inquisitive reader with the means of detection. And it is hard to conceive that, if an error had been committed in the position of his semicircle, it should never be detected by Stephens himself, or suggested to him by his friends or enemies. This, however, will appear less improbable if we attend to the following consideration, that Stephens returned his MSS. at least as soon as he had completed his edition of 1550, perhaps as soon as he had finished his collations. For when he presented a copy of that edition, immediately after it was printed, to the divines of the Sorbonne, and they required him to produce a MS. with which they might compare it, he answered that his MSS. had already been returned to the Royal Library. If, in the short and turbulent interval between that conference and his migration from Paris, from which city he was driven by the malice of his persecutors, he had discovered in his Greek Testament the unprecedented reading, which omits ἐν τῷ οὐρανῷ while it retains the rest of the disputed passage, he would naturally consult his book of collations, which would only confirm the printed copy; for, in those collations, it is probable that the mistake first arose.

"To draw a decisive conclusion from the above-mentioned facts, would require no small skill, in weighing and balancing opposite probabilities; and there is one material part of the evidence, which, from its nature, is not easily to be appreciated, but by persons who have had much experience in the collation of MSS. I mean that part which relates to the proof of identity from the coincidence of readings. However, the best critics unanimously agree in the opinion, that Stephens's MSS. had not the disputed passage; and among these Mill and Bengelius, whose orthodoxy is not doubted, and who were convinced of its authenticity." *

After going over the Greek fathers seriatim, he thus sums up his account of them.

* Christian Observer, Vol. VI. pp. 227, 228.

"On a review of the Greek fathers, we discover no proof that any of them were acquainted with the disputed passage. The omission of it in Justin Martyr, in the Adumbrations attributed to Clemens Alexandrinus, in the Epistle of the Bishops at Sardis, in the Sixty-second Oration of Epiphanius, in the Treatises on the Holy Spirit by Basil, Gregory Nazianzen, and Didymus, is hardly to be reconciled with the supposition that they had it in their copies. And Cyril clearly either had it not, or suspected its authenticity. And though we might allow the omission in a single father to arise from some unknown cause, yet the universal silence of all the early Greek writers forms a presumption against its authenticity, to which I know not what can be opposed, unless it be suggested that they understood the words *these three are one* as relating merely to unity of testimony, not of essence; and therefore thought that no argument for the doctrine of the Trinity could be built upon it. But does it appear that they actually put such a construction upon these words? Is there any trace of such an interpretation in their works? Or is it at all probable from analogy, that they would unanimously refuse the aid of a passage, which almost all modern defenders of the Trinity have employed without scruple?

"Even if these fathers approved the interpretation above mentioned, it remains still to be shown, why they never quoted 1 John v. 7 in proof of a trinity of persons, or as an example of Christ being called The WORD." *

After examining very carefully the several Latin fathers who quote or allude to this verse, he thus sums up his account of their testimony.

"From the foregoing extracts it is evident that the Latin fathers are more favorable than the Greek to the authenticity of 1 John v. 7. For while not a single quotation or clear

* Christian Observer, Vol. VI. p. 289.

allusion to it is found among the latter, for the first thirteen centuries, we discover a reference to it in the third century by Cyprian, and in the fifth, express quotations by Fulgentius, and the author of the African Confession; in the sixth, by Cassiodorus; in the eighth, by Etherius and Beatus. And is not their positive testimony of greater weight than the merely negative testimony, the silence, of any number of Greek or Latin fathers? It may be difficult indeed to account for their silence upon the supposition that they were acquainted with the disputed passage. Yet, if a single witness of unsuspected veracity affirm that it existed in his copy, his testimony may outweigh the argument drawn from the mere silence of great numbers. Since, therefore, a Latin writer of the third century has referred to it, will not his authority counterbalance the negative testimony of all the Greek fathers?

"Many of the orthodox have thought so, and the anxious desire which some writers have shown to set aside this evidence by the arbitrary and unsatisfactory hypothesis, that Cyprian's reference was to the eighth verse and not to the seventh, implies that they felt the superior force of affirmative testimony. For my own part, I freely confess that if Cyprian had affirmed that the seventh verse existed in his Greek copy, I should have paid very little regard to the omission of it by other fathers of the same or a later century. But, is this the case? or have we any evidence that he was in possession of a single Greek copy of St. John's Epistle; or that he could even read Greek; or that, if he could read it, he valued the Greek copies more than the Latin?

"Till these questions are answered in the affirmative, all that we can infer from his quotation is, that the testimony of the heavenly witnesses was in his Latin copy. And although that version, from its high antiquity, is deserving of great respect; yet, among the innumerable and discordant translations into the Latin, it is possible that the disputed passage might be interpolated in some copies as early as the age of Cyprian, and of course in those of Fulgentius, Vigilius, Cassiodorus, Etherius, and Beatus, though unknown to Augustine, Jerome, Eucherius, Facundus, and Bede.

"When we reflect that the Latin fathers do not quote this passage uniformly, either with respect to the words or the order of the verses, it is natural to conclude that their guide was not the Greek Original, but the Latin Version; in the MSS. of which the same varieties have been observed.

"Though the charge of interpolation may be thought a very serious one, much will depend upon the manner and the motive. He who first inserted the seventh verse in the margin of the Latin version, probably had no intention of imposing upon the reader by giving his own comment for the word of God. And when afterwards it obtained a place in the text, the transcriber probably had no doubt but that he was restoring a passage, which the former copyist having through inadvertence omitted, upon the discovery of his mistake had inserted in the margin, for want of convenient space in the text.

"It is urged that the verse must be genuine because an interpolation of such magnitude and importance would have been speedily detected and loudly complained of by the Arians. But may we not on the other hand, with equal plausibility, contend that if a passage so decisively in favor of the doctrine of the Trinity had been left out of the copies of St. John's First Epistle, the omission would have been immediately discovered by the orthodox, and charged upon their adversaries? Since then we find no complaints of this sort in the ancient writers of either party, it is plain that no inference can be drawn from a silence for which, on both suppositions, it is alike difficult to assign a probable cause." *

I have observed, what I had not attended to till the preceding sheets were printed, as my copy of Mr. Charles Butler's *Horæ Biblicæ* is contained in his Miscellaneous Works,† published in 1817, that his "Short Historical Outline of the Disputes respecting the Authenticity of the Verse of the Three Heavenly Witnesses" was first published in 1805; some time before the two works which have just been noticed. It is contained in two Letters "to the Rev. Herbert Marsh," and constitutes the second Appendix to the very interesting work of Mr. Butler, which is known to every scholar.‡ It illustrates the extensive reading, the patient research, and the great suavity which distinguish all the productions of one of the oldest and most voluminous writers of the present day.

This short outline gives a more brief view of the Controversy than has been presented in these papers, and omits many things which have been introduced in them. There are also a few inaccuracies which I have noticed, though they are not of any material importance. The plan which Mr. Butler pursues is the following. He gives,

I. Some account of the state of the question; II. Of the history of the general admission of The Verse into the printed text; III. And of the principal disputes to which it has given rise; IV. An inquiry whether the general sense of the text is affected by the omission of The Verse; V. Some account

* Christian Observer, pp. 354, 355.

† [The correct title is "Philological and Biographical Works," of which the *Horæ Biblicæ* forms Vol. I.—Ed.]

‡ [This "Historical Outline" is reprinted in Vol. II. of Sparks's "Collection of Essays and Tracts in Theology," Boston, 1823.—Ed.]

of the argument in favor of its authenticity from prescription; VI. Some account of the arguments against it from its absence from the Greek manuscripts; VII. Of the answers to those arguments, from its supposed existence in the manuscripts of Valla; VIII. From its supposed existence in the manuscripts of the Complutensian editors; IX. And from its supposed existence in the manuscripts used by Robert Stephens; X. Some observations on the argument arising on its not being inserted in the Apostolos or Collection of Epistles read in the Greek Church; XI. On its not being inserted in the Oriental versions; XII. On its not being inserted in the most ancient Latin manuscripts; XIII. On the silence of all the Greek fathers respecting it; XIV. On the silence of the most ancient of the Latin fathers respecting it; XV. Some account is then given of what has been written respecting its first introduction into the Greek and Latin manuscripts.

Under these general topics, almost everything of importance in the controversy is noticed. Were I to go over them, it would be to repeat a great deal of what has been already stated. He gives the evidence *pro* and *con* with great candor and accuracy; but lays more stress on several points than I conceive they will fairly bear. One or two passages deserve to be quoted for the information which they contain. As a Catholic, he feels himself in some difficulty from the Decree of the Council of Trent, which pronounces the authenticity and correctness of the Latin Vulgate. The following passage explains the process by which a good Catholic may escape from the anathema of the Council, though he may dispute the authenticity of this verse. Dr. Geddes would have cut the knot which Mr. Butler's reasoning does not unloose.

"Here the communicant with the see of Rome takes an higher ground. The Council of Trent, Session 4, declared anathema to all 'who should not receive for holy and canonical, all and every part of the Books of the Old and New Testament, as they had been accustomably read in the Catholic Church, and as they stood in the old vulgate edition:' And in the sixth session, declared 'the Vulgate to be authentic, and that no one should, on any pretence, dare or presume to reject it.'

"Now, when the Council of Trent made this decree, The Verse had long been accustomably read in the Catholic Church, and long made a part in the old vulgate edition; those, therefore, in communion with the see of Rome, who now reject The Verse, fall within the Council's anathema.

"To these objections the adversaries of The Verse reply:

"1st, That, in the times of which we are now speaking, there was little of biblical criticism, and that no works of those times have reached us, in which such an objection either would be made, or would be noticed.

"2dly, That, before too great a stress is laid on its insertion in the Vulgate, an accurate notion should be formed of the edition denoted, in these cases, by the appellation of the Latin Vulgate. It does not denote the edition, anterior to St. Jerome, which, from its superior celebrity, was called the Ancient Italic; it does not denote the edition published by St. Jerome; it merely denotes that edition, which, at the time of the Council of Trent, was generally in use; and afterwards served as the ground-work of the editions published, first by Sixtus Quintus, afterwards by Clement the Eighth, and which last edition is the archetype of the modern Vulgate: that this edition partook more of the modern than of ancient versions; and that, standing by itself, it is, in a matter of criticism, of no authority.

"3dly, To suppose that the Council of Trent pronounced the Vulgate to be wholly free from error, and that no one was t liberty to vary from it, in translation or exposition, is going to an extreme. In declaring it to be authentic, the Council did not declare the Vulgate to be inspired or infallible; he Council only pronounced it to be inerrant, where the dogmata of faith or morals are concerned. In this decision every Roman Catholic must acquiesce, as he receives the Scripture from the Church, under her authority, and with her nterpretation; but further than this, the Council leaves the Vulgate, in mere matters of criticism, to the private judgment of every individual. To this effect Father Salmeron, who was one of the ten first disciples of St. Ignatius, and who assisted at the Council of Trent in the character of one of the Pope's theologians, is cited by the Abbé de Vence, to have expressed himself in the third of his prolegomena."*

Mr. Butler does not seem quite satisfied with this reasoning, and hence he introduces Bossuet, who speaks in a much higher tone of authority.

"In this stage of the argument, Bossuet takes very high ground in one of his letters to Leibniz, published by Mr. Dutens, in his edition of Leibniz's works; as, in that letter, Bossuet seems to place the general acquiescence of the Roman Catholic Church in the authenticity of The Verse, among the traditions which the Church receives, and the faithful are therefore bound to adopt. As everything which has fallen from the pen of that great man is important, and the passage in question is little known, it is here transcribed at length.

"'J'avoue au reste, Monsieur, ce vous dites des anciens exemplaires Grecs sur le passage, *Tres sunt, &c.;* mais vous sçavez aussi-bien que moi, que l'article contenu dans ce passage ne doit pas être pour cela révoqué en doute, étant d'ail-

* Pp. 383-385.

leurs établi, non-seulement *par la Tradition des Eglises*, mai encore par l'Ecriture très évidemment. Vous sçavez auss sans doute, que ce passage se trouve reçu dans tout l'Occi-dent; ce qui paroît manifeste, sans même remonter plus haut par la production qu'en fait S. Fulgence dans ses Ecrits, & même dans une excellente Confession de foi présentée unani-mément au Roi Huneric par toute l'Eglise d'Afrique. C· témoignage produit par un aussi grand Théologien, & pa cette sçavante Eglise, n'ayant point été reproché par les héré-tiques, & au contraire étant confirmé par le sang de tant d martyrs, et encore par tant de miracles, dont cette Confessio de foi fut suivie, est une démonstration de la Tradition, du moins de toute l'Eglise d'Afrique, l'une des plus illustre du monde. On trouve même dans S. Cyprien une allu-sion manifeste à ce passage, qui a passé naturellement dan notre Vulgate, & confirme la Tradition de tout l'Occiden Je suis, &c.

"'† J. Benigne, *Evêque de Meaux*.'" *

* Pp. 384, 385. [That is: — "I acknowledge moreover, Sir, the trutl of what you say respecting the ancient Greek copies on the passage, *Ther are three*, &c.; but you know as well as I do, that the article of faith con-tained in this passage ought not to be called in question on that account being otherwise established, not only *by the tradition of the churches*, bu very evidently by Scripture. You also know, without doubt, that thi passage has been received throughout the entire West; which is shown without going further back, by its citation in the writings of St. Fulgen-tius, and even in an excellent Confession of Faith unanimously presente to King Huneric by the whole African Church. This testimony, produce by so great a theologian, and by this learned Church, having not been ob-jected to by the heretics, and, on the contrary, having been confirmed by the blood of so many martyrs, and still further by so many miracles fol-lowing this Confession of Faith, is a demonstration of the tradition at least of the whole African Church, one of the most illustrious in the world. We find even in Saint Cyprian a manifest allusion to this passage, which naturally passed into our Vulgate, and confirms the tradition of the whole West. I am, &c.,

"† J. Benigne, *Bishop of Meaux*."]

Tradition is no canon of criticism, and can therefore prove nothing in matters where parchment and ink are the only authorities. Mr. Butler, with his characteristic caution, does not give his own opinion on this curious, and, to all well-informed men, unsatisfactory mode of reasoning; nor does he give a positive opinion on the spuriousness or authenticity of the verse in question. He leaves the reader to guess whether he doubts as a critic, but believes as a Catholic.

On another point a passage of some importance occurs, and which has also a bearing on the critical authority of the received and *infallibly* ascertained text of the Vulgate.

"The adversaries of The Verse contend that—IT IS WANTING IN FORTY OF THE MOST ANCIENT MANUSCRIPTS OF THE LATIN VERSION. This, they say, equipoises, if it do not overbalance the authority of those Latin manuscripts in which it is contained.

"In 1743, Sabatier published, at Rheims, his "Bibliorum sacrorum Latinæ versiones antiquæ, seu vetus Italica, et ceteræ quæcunquè in codicibus Manuscriptis reperiri potuerunt, quæ cum vulgatâ Latinâ et cum textu Græco comparantur." The object of the work is to restore the text of the ancient Italic by putting together the quotations of the Bible in the works of the ancient fathers; where none can be found, Sabatier supplies the chasm from the Vulgate. He was so fortunate as to find, in different parts of the works of St. Augustin, a sufficient number of quotations to form the whole of the first four chapters, and likewise the beginning of the fifth. But, when he comes to the seventh verse, this very voluminous father, who wrote not less than ten treatises on the Epistle in question, suddenly deserts him, though immediately after this critical place, he comes again to his assistance. This chasm, therefore, Sabatier fills up by a quotation from Vigilius Tapsensis, who wrote at the end of the fifth century." *

This fact is, I conceive, of great importance. It shows very clearly, that even in the writings of the Latin fathers, till the fifth century, beside being wanting in many of the best and oldest MSS., the verse did not exist.

Mr. Butler thinks that the principal argument in favor of the verse, which has not been satisfactorily answered, is its having a place in the Confession of Faith, presented by the African Bishops to Huneric. This is part of the controversy between Travis and Porson, in which Mr. Butler thinks the latter displayed his wit more than his logic or learning. His own argument on that passage in the creed, however, appears to me very inconclusive. It is full of supposition and hypothesis. But as this topic will occur again in our notice of Bishop Burgess's publications, we shall advert to it no further at present.

The valuable work of the late Bishop Middleton on the Greek Article, which was published in 1808, contains a long and learned note, or rather disquisition, on this passage. This volume displays more profound learning, laborious investigation, and critical acumen, than any critical or philological work on the New Testament published in this country during the present century. It is impossible too highly to estimate its value as an aid to the critical interpretation of the New Testament. Independently of the labored and philosophical discussion of the doctrine of the Article, the application of the doctrine to the interpretation of many important passages has enabled the learned author to throw much light upon them. The way in which Dr. Middleton was led into a discussion on the disputed passage, he thus explains: —

* Pp. 395, 396.

"It has been insisted, that the omission of the rejected passage rather embarrasses the context: Bengel regards the two verses as being connected '*adamantinâ cohærentiâ:*' and yet, it must be allowed, that among the various interpretations there are some which will at least endure the absence of the seventh verse. But the difficulty to which the present undertaking has directed my attention is of another kind: it respects the Article in εἰς τὸ ἕν in the final clause of the eighth verse: if the seventh verse had not been spurious, nothing could have been plainer than that TO ἕν of verse 8 referred to ἕν of verse 7: as the case now stands, I do not perceive the force or meaning of the article; and the same difficulty is briefly noticed by Wolfius. In order to prove that this is not merely *nodum in scirpo quærere*, I think it right to examine at some length what are the occasions on which before εἷς the article may be inserted." *

The nature of the argument which is pursued, in order to account for the use of the article in the eighth verse, cannot be understood unless I were to quote, what is impossible, the whole dissertation. Nor is it necessary I should do so, as Dr. Middleton himself is unable satisfactorily to account for the occurrence of the article in the 8th verse consistently with his doctrine, nor can he, on the other hand, satisfactorily get rid of it. His own convictions seem, on the whole, to have been unfavorable to the authority of the verse, and yet he thinks the matter not yet entirely decided.

"In concluding this note," he says, "I think it right to offer something towards its vindication. I am not ignorant, that in the rejection of the controverted passage learned and good men are now, for the most part, agreed; and I contemplate with admiration and delight the gigantic exertions of intellect which have established this acquiescence: the

* Pp. 633, 634.

objection, however, which has given rise to this discussion, I could not consistently with my plan suppress. On the whole, I am led to suspect, that though so much labor and critical acuteness have been bestowed on these celebrated verses, more is yet to be done before the mystery in which they are involved can be wholly developed." *

Much as I respect the learning and talents of Bishop Middleton, I cannot allow that a difficulty, which may belong to the use of the article by one of the inspired writers, and he by no means invariably correct in his Greek phraseology, ought materially to affect our judgment of the readings on which an accurate text of the Scriptures must be founded. Such difficulties may be a kind of subsidiary evidence on one side or another; but can be no satisfactory proof of the real reading. It is but justice to Dr. Middleton to say, that it is only on this ground that he argues; for though he conceives that something additional may yet be brought forward on the disputed verse, the evident leaning of his mind was to the evidence in opposition to its authenticity.

The controversy experienced a temporary revival in 1809 and 1810, by the appearance of an article in the Eclectic Review. This able paper, which I believe I am justified in ascribing to the pen of the Rev. Dr. J. P. Smith, of Homerton, is a review of the Improved Version of the New Testament, by some anonymous Unitarians. The disputed passage here passes under review, in noticing the text from which the Improved Version had been formed. In reference to it, the learned writer says, "It is found in NO Greek MS., ancient or recent, except one to which we shall presently advert;—in no ancient version, being interpolated only in the later transcripts of the Vulgate. Not one of the *Greek* fathers

* Pp. 652, 653.

recognizes it, though many of them collect every species and shadow of argument, down to the most allegorical and shockingly ridiculous, in favor of the doctrine of the Trinity, — though they often cite the words immediately contiguous, both before and after, — and though, with immense labor and art, they extract from the next words the very sense which this passage has in following times been adduced to furnish. Of the *Latin* fathers, not one has quoted it, till Eucherius, of Lyons, in the middle of the fifth century; and in his works there is much reason to believe that it has been interpolated."*

The expression of this opinion roused the indignation of an individual, who had more zeal than knowledge. Shortly after there appeared "The Critique in the Eclectic Review, on 1 John v. 7, confuted by Martin's Examination of Emlyn's Answer; to which is added, an Appendix, containing remarks on Mr. Porson's Letters to Archdeacon Travis. By J. Pharez." 8vo. 1809. To this feeble champion of a lost cause, the learned reviewer rejoined, in two able papers in the months of January and February, 1810. After going through the several steps of the argument in a very lucid and masterly manner, he thus characterizes this production of the Dunciad: — "The pamphlet which has led us to this discussion must be allowed to be an extraordinary production. A Greek motto on the title-page is so happily managed, as to suggest shrewd proof that the writer cannot construe a line of that language. Grossly destitute of literature, and the very lowest principles of critical science, he assaults the greatest critic in Europe, and sings aloud his self-complacent triumph. Actually ignorant *what words* are deemed spurious, and what are held to be genuine, and equally ignorant on the

* Eclectic Review, Vol. V. p. 248.

nature of the evidence and the minor points of the case, he blunders through page after page with the most comfortable fatuity. He truly deserves our pity; but as to feeling angry with him, it is quite impossible." *

In 1810, the publication of a British edition of Griesbach's Greek Testament, in an appendix to the second volume of which is a valuable dissertation on 1 John v. 7, brought more generally before British scholars the judgment and reasonings of that distinguished critic. It contains a succinct and correct statement of the whole case, which is decidedly unfavorable to the authenticity of the verse. The substance of the dissertation is, that the text is not found in any Greek MS. except one of very recent date, — that it is not quoted by any Greek father, — and that it rests chiefly on the authority of Vigilius Tapsensis. He sums up his discussion by saying, "If vouchers so few, doubtful, suspected, and recent, and arguments so trifling, could suffice to establish the genuineness of any reading, in opposition to so many weighty testimonies and arguments, there would no longer be any criterion of truth and falsehood in criticism, and the whole text of the New Testament would become wholly uncertain and doubtful."

The authority of Griesbach in matters of criticism stands deservedly high. His doctrinal sentiments are not suspected of heterodoxy, his candor is generally acknowledged; and of his learning, laborious diligence and soundness of judgment, there can be but one opinion among competent judges. The influence of his decisions on the correctness of any reading may therefore be expected to be great. Indeed, I question whether the authority of any text, which he has decidedly rejected, is likely to be restored. Doubts, it is true, exist re-

* Eclectic Review, Vol. VI. p. 162.

specting his mode of classifying the MSS. of the Greek Testament, and something very formidable has been adduced both by Laurence and Nolan against his whole system of recensions; but I do not know that the results, as to the text, will be materially different, though a very different system of classification should be adopted. His judgment as to the age and authority of the various MSS. which have been examined, and of the collateral evidence, is likely to stand the test of the most rigorous examination.

Previously to entering on the controversy in which Dr. Burgess, formerly Bishop of St. David's, now of Salisbury, has been so long engaged, and which still continues, it may be proper to notice several works in which the subject occupies a prominent place, though it is a secondary, and not the primary object. Such, however, is the importance attached to the authority of this passage by the writers, that it is not going too far, perhaps, to say, that had not this passage, and one or two others, been concerned, the volumes we are about to refer to would never, probably, have been written. They form an additional illustration of the manner in which the controversy has branched off into other subjects.

The first of these works which deserves attention is one of great labor and research. "An Inquiry into the Integrity of the Greek Vulgate, or Received Text of the New Testament: in which the Greek Manuscripts are newly classed, the Integrity of the authorized Text vindicated, and the various Readings traced to their Origin. By the Rev. Frederick Nolan, a Presbyter of the United Church." London. 1815. The leading object of Mr. Nolan's work is to maintain the integrity or correctness of the common Greek text against the objections of Griesbach, and especially to overthrow his classification of the Manuscripts. He has done a good deal to shake the fabric on which the learned German has constructed his ingenious system of classification; but not much to establish the immaculate purity of the common text. After making, in his preface, some objections to the elaborate theories of those who maintain the imperfections of the text, he proceeds to state his own theory, or plan of defence, and the arrangement of his work.

"On these grounds the first notion was formed by the author of the following pages, that an Inquiry into the history of the sacred text would most probably lead to the perfect vindication of the vulgar edition. He was encouraged in this expectation by the effect which he perceived a few facts had in solving some of the greatest difficulties which embarrassed its history. At two periods only could he perceive the possibility of the ecclesiastical tradition having been interrupted; during the ascendancy of the Arian party under Constantine, and on its suppression under the elder Theodosius. The destruction of the sacred books in the Dioclesian persecution, and the revisal of the sacred text by Eusebius, furnished an adequate solution of the greatest difficulty which arose, from the varieties in the copies of the original text, and of the translations which differ from the Greek Vulgate.

"To this point, of consequence, his first attention is turned; and it forms the subject of the first section of the following Inquiry. He has thence endeavored to show that the coincidence between the Eastern and Western texts, on which the credit of the Corrected Edition is rested, must be attributed to the influence of Eusebius's revisal, which was published under the auspices of the Emperor Constantine.

"Thus far, however, a negative argument is deduced in favor of the Received Text. The character of this text still remains to be investigated: to this point the author next directs his attention, and he prosecutes it through the two following sections. As the integrity and purity of the Greek and Latin Churches render their testimony of the highest authority in ascertaining the genuine text; on their joint authority he has consequently ventured to distribute the Greek Manuscripts into Classes; and to vindicate that particular class of text which exists in the vulgar edition.

"From the ground thus taken up, the whole subject may be commanded almost at a glance. In the following sections, the tradition of the Greek and Latin Churches is carefully traced from the apostolical age; and on the concurring or relative testimony of those witnesses, the general and doctrinal integrity of the Received Text is established. In vindication of the verbal integrity of this text, the evidence of the Syriac Church is called in; and on the joint testimony of the primitive Version of this Church, and the primitive Italic, a decisive argument is finally deduced in favor of the antiquity of the Greek Vulgate.

"In the last section, the author has endeavored to point out the particular manner in which the remaining Classes of Text, into which the Greek Manuscripts are distributed, have originated from a corruption of the vulgar edition. The whole of the diversities in those manuscripts are traced to three revisals of the sacred text, which were published in Egypt, Palestine, and Constantinople. The number of various readings is thence easily accounted for; and a solution offered of some objections which are raised to the doctrinal and verbal integrity of the Received Text or Vulgar edition.

"From this brief sketch of the plan of the work, the reader will easily comprehend in what manner the author has avoided those consequences which he charges on the systems of his opponents: and how the integrity of the Received Text may be established independent of the objections which lie against the Corrected Edition. An interruption in the tradition, by which the former text is supported, is admitted to have taken place, when the scripture canon was revised by Eusebius, and the Church became subject to the dominion of the Arians. But the tradition is carried *above* this period, which did not exceed forty years, and the Received Text proved to have existed previously, by its coincidence with those Versions of the Oriental and Western Churches which were made *before* the text was revised by Eusebius. So that, although the tradition has been interrupted for this inconsiderable period, it has remained as unsophisticated in the two centuries which preceded Constantine's age, as in the last fourteen, during which it has confessedly remained uncorrupted." *

All this may seem very plausible, and is very ingeniously supported by the learned author; but it is one of the purest hypotheses ever devised to support a favorite idea. It ascribes a great deal too much to the tradition of churches; assumes that they took more pains to preserve or to corrupt the text than there is any reason to believe they ever did; and refers to revisals and editions, almost as if he were speaking of printed works. He contends for what I conceive to be a very objectionable position, — the doctrinal purity of a church, as the guaranty of the purity of the text of Scripture, instead of the text preserved by the providence of God, the great means of correcting the errors and guiding the opinions of all churches. Mr. Nolan certainly does not intend to serve the cause of Popery, but there is something in his argument which a learned Roman Catholic would consider as very favorable to one of the leading doctrines of his church, — the authority of ecclesiastical tradition.

It is not my business, however, to pronounce upon the general merits of Mr. Nolan's work further than they have

* Nolan's Inquiry, Pref. pp. xii. - xv.

relation to the subject of our Memoir. I consider Gries-.ch's classification of MSS. arbitrary and hypothetical; I ιve the same opinion of Nolan's hypothesis, which is placed opposition to it. He has succeeded in demolishing the bric of his opponent, but not in establishing his own. The tegrity or incorrectness of the Greek text must be proved disproved by facts and reasonings, independent of all such hemes.

Mr. Nolan abandons the authority of the Greek MSS. and e Greek Church in support of the disputed passage, and sts its defence entirely on that of the Latin or African hurch. I cannot give the whole of his argument, but the llowing passage, I think, contains everything of importance it.

"With respect to 1 John v. 7. the case is materially differ-ıt. If this verse be received, it must be admitted on the ngle testimony of the Western Church; as far at least as spects the external evidence. And though it may seem nwarrantable to set aside the authority of the Greek Church, nd pay exclusive respect to the Latin, where a question rises on the authenticity of a passage which properly belongs the text of the former; yet, when the doctrine inculcated that passage is taken into account, there may be good rea-on for giving even a preference to the Western Church over hat of the Eastern. The former was uncorrupted by the eresy of the Arians, who rejected the doctrine of the pas-age in question; the latter was wholly resigned to that eresy for at least forty years, while the Western Church etained its purity. And while the testimony borne by the atter on the subject before us is consistent and full, that orne by the former is internally defective. It is delivered n language which has not even the merit of being grammat-cally correct; while the testimony of the latter is not only unexceptionable in itself, but possesses the singular merit of removing the forementioned imperfection, on being merely turned into Greek, and inserted in the context of the original. Under these circumstances there seems to be little reasonableness in allowing the Western Church any authority, and denying it, in this instance, a preference over the Eastern.

"But numberless circumstances conspire to strengthen the authority of the Latin Church in supporting the authenticity of this passage. The particular Church on whose testimony principally we receive the disputed verse, is that of Africa. And even at the first sight, it must be evident, that the most implicit respect is due to its testimony.

"1. In those great convulsions which agitated the Eastern and Western Churches for eight years, with scarcely any intermission; and which subjected the sacred text to the greatest changes, through that vast tract of country which extends round the Levant, from Libya to Illyricum, the African provinces were exposed to the horrors of persecution but for an inconsiderable period. The Church, of course, which was established in this region, neither required a new supply of sacred books, nor received those which had been revised by Eusebius and St. Jerome; as removed out of the range of the influence of those ancient fathers.

"2. As the African Church possessed this competency to deliver a pure unsophisticated testimony on the subject before us; that which it has borne is as explicit as it is plenary: since it is delivered in a Confession prepared by the whole Church assembled in council. After the African provinces had been overrun by the Vandals, Hunerick, their king, summoned the bishops of this Church, and of the adjacent isles, to deliberate on the doctrine inculcated in the disputed passage. Between three and four hundred prelates attended the Council, which met at Carthage; and Eugenius, as bishop of that see, drew up the Confession of the orthodox, in which the contested verse is expressly quoted. That a whole church should thus concur in quoting a verse which was not contained in the received text, is wholly inconceivable: and admitting that 1 John v. 7 was thus generally received, its universal prevalence in that text is only to be accounted for by supposing it to have existed in it from the beginning.

"3. The testimony which the African Church has borne on the subject before us is not more strongly recommended by the universal consent, than the immemorial tradition of the evidence which attests the authenticity of the contested passage. Victor Vitensis and Fulgentius, Marcus Celedensis, St. Cyprian, and Tertullian, were Africans, and have referred to the verse before us. Of these witnesses, which follow each other at almost equal intervals, the first is referred to the age of Eugenius, the last to that nearly of the Apostles. They thus form a traditionary chain, carrying up the testimony of the African Church until it loses itself in time immemorial.

"4. The testimony of the African Church, which possesses these strong recommendations, receives confirmation from the corroborating evidence of other churches, which were similarly circumstanced. Phœbadius and Eucherius, the latter of whom had been translated from the Spanish to the Gallican Church, were members of the latter; and both these churches had been exempt, not less than the African, from the effects of Diocletian's persecution. Both these early fathers, Phœbadius and Eucherius, attest the authenticity of the contested passage: the testimony of the former is entitled to the greater respect, as he boldly withstood the authority of Hosius, whose influence tended to extend the Arian opinions in the Western World, at the very period in which he cited the contested passage. In addition to these witnesses, we have, in the testimony of Maximus, the evidence of a person who visited the African Church; and who there becoming acquainted with the disputed passage, wrote a tract for the purpose of employing it against the Arians. The testimony of these witnesses forms a valuable accession to that of the African Church.

"5. We may appeal to the testimony of the Greek Church in confirmation of the African Churches. Not to insist at present on positive testimonies, the disputed verse, though not supported by the *text* of the original Greek, is clearly supported by its *context*. The latter does not agree so well with itself, as it does with the testimony of the African Church. The grammatical structure, which is imperfect in itself, directly recovers its original integrity on being filled up with the passage which is offered on the testimony of this witness. Thus far the testimony of the Greek Church is plainly corroborative of that of the Western.

"6. In fine, as Origen and Eusebius have both thought that one church becomes a sufficient voucher for one even of the *sacred books* of the Canon; and as Eusebius has borne the most unqualified evidence to the integrity and purity of the Church of Africa, we can have no just grounds for rejecting its testimony, on *a single verse* of Scripture. And when we consider the weight of the argument arising in favor of this verse from the internal evidence; how forcibly the subject of it was pressed upon the attention of St. John; and how amply it is attested by that external evidence which is antecedent, though deficient in that which is subsequent to the times of the Apostles, our conviction must rise that this passage is authentic. But when we add the very obvious solution which this want of subsequent evidence receives from the probability that Eusebius suppressed this passage in the edition which he revised; and which became the received text of the Church, which remained in subjection to the Arians for the forty years that succeeded; I trust nothing further can be wanting to convince any ingenuous mind that 1 John v. 7 really proceeded from St. John the Evangelist." *

The notes of the author on this passage, which I cannot quote, add some additional weight to his argument, and throw some light on parts of his text, which to general readers must appear obscure: but I cannot help again saying, that to maintain the purity of the text of Scripture by the testimony of any church is dangerous ground. To refer to confessions of faith in proof of what must have been the reading of the sacred text while the readings of MSS. of the Scriptures preserved by that very church are not in unison with the confession, is a very clumsy mode of establishing the point. That Eusebius possessed the power, or the disposition, to alter the sacred text; or that any alteration made by him should have found its way into all existing Greek MSS., is altogether improbable, or at least destitute of any adequate support.

Although I consider that Mr. Nolan fails in maintaining the common reading in 1 John v. 7, and in supporting his hypotheses generally, it is due to him to say, that his work contains much that is worthy of attention from the biblical scholar, and is written throughout in a very commendable spirit of moderation and candor. That I may not be considered as keeping back anything which belongs to the other side of the question from what I espouse, I extract the following note, in which Mr. Nolan gives some account of the reading of the ancient French and Waldensian versions.

"Of the old versions which have been published in French, two were made by the Waldenses; vid. Le Long, Bibl. Sacr. Tom. I. p. 313, col. 2. e. Morland on the Church of the Val-

* Pp. 293 - 305.

leys, p. 14. But one copy of this version has fallen into my hands, which was printed at the native place of Peter Waldo; 'Au Lyon, l'an de grace 1521.' The following is the reading of 1 Joh. v. 7, 8. fol. clxiv. b. 'Trois choses sont qui donnent tesmoing au ciel, le pere le filz et le sainct esperit, et ces trois sont une chose. Et trois choses qui donnent tesmoing en terre, esperit eaue et sang.' This testimony would be of little importance until the character of the translation was investigated by a comparison with other French Versions and the old Italic and modern Latin Vulgate; were it not for the following considerations: (1.) It *differs* from the Latin Vulgate; as it reads 'le filz' for 'Verbum.' (2.) It *agrees* in this reading with an ancient Confession of Faith, used by the Waldenses. Leger, Hist. Gen. des Eglis. Vaudois, P. I. ch. viii. p. 50. ed. Leyd. 1669. Eschant. v. de *la Doctrine des Vaudois*, contenant la fidele traduction de l'Exposition qu'ils ont donné au Symbole des Apôtres — où ils en prouvent tous les Articles *par passages exprès de la S. Ecriture.* — Lequel Dieu est un Trinité, *comme il est ecrit* en la Loy, 'O Israel écoute,' &c. — Et *S. Jean*, *'Il y en a trois qui rendent témoinage au ciel, le Pere, le Fils, et le S. Esprit, et ces trois sont un.'* The original of this passage, as far as I can gather from M. Leger, may be found in le Sieur du Perrin, Hist. des Vaudois et Albigeois, chap. v. p. 201. sqq. The proof appears to me to be so far complete, that this passage was adopted in the authorized text used by the Waldenses. The following considerations seem adequate to evince that it existed in the Latin Version revised by St. Eusebius of Vercelli, who published the old translation which prevailed in the Italic Diocese. (1.) In reading 'Filius,' it agrees with Tertullian and Cyprian, against the common testimony of the Modern Vulgate, and the Latin Fathers; vid. infr. p. 291. n. sqq. (2.) St. Eusebius might have hence adopted this reading, as he has adopted other readings from those fathers, in his revisal: vid. infr. p. 146. n. (3.) The French version agrees with the old Italic in possessing other readings derived from the same source: in the Lord's Prayer, we find, instead of 'ne inducas nos in temptationem,' *Lat. Vulg.*, 'ne nous mene mye en temptacion, *cest a dire ne souffre mye que nous syonz temptez'*: conformably to Tertullian and Cyprian: vid. infr. p. 330. n. (4.) The disputed passage, as read in the Waldensian Confession, and the French Version, is accommodated to the state of religious opinion which prevailed in the age of St. Eusebius. By changing Verbum to Filius, in vers. 7. the Sabellian evasion of the passage was obviated: vid. infr. p. 539. n. By cutting off 'et hi tres (in) unum sunt,' in vers. 8. the Arian evasion of the passsage was equally obviated. For this phrase furnished some countenance to the notion of those heretics who asserted that 'unum sunt' signified an unity, not of substance, but of will and testimony. As these are coincidences which the Waldenses cannot be supposed to have created, I thence conclude, that 1 John v. 7. not only existed in the revisal of the old Italic Version made by Eusebius Vercellensis; but that the peculiar reading of this text, which is found in the French Version, and which has excited M. Porson's notice, has been thus remotely adopted from St. Cyprian: vid. Porson. Lett. to Trav. p. 377. It thus easily made its way into Wicklef's translation, through the Lollards, who were disciples of the Waldenses; vid. Pors. ibid. Morl. ub. supr. p. 184."*

The work of Mr. Nolan occasioned a controversy in the Christian Remembrancer for 1822, between that gentleman and the Rev. John Oxlee. It was carried on, as discussions

* Pref. pp. xviii., xix.

of this nature in periodical works usually are, with a good deal of warmth, but without the names of the parties appearing. It led at last to the publication of the following pamphlet: "Three Letters addressed to the Rev. Frederic Nolan, Vicar of Prittlewell, on his erroneous Criticisms and Mis-statements in the Christian Remembrancer, relative to the Text of the Heavenly Witnesses; in which are contained, also, Strictures on the Vindication of the spurious Passage by the Bishop of St. David's: together with a new Translation of the Genuine Text, proposed and defended from every Cavil. By the Rev. John Oxlee, Rector of Scawton, and Curate of Stonegrave." York. 1825.

At present I shall postpone any notice of the debate with Dr. Burgess, till we come to that period of the controversy in which the Bishop is more particularly concerned, when Mr. Oxlee again appears; nor shall I say anything of the style in which Mr. Oxlee has treated his opponent. His language is that of unmeasured severity and contempt. To this he appears to have been provoked by some things said by Mr. Nolan; but scarcely anything can justify the language which he has, in several places, employed. He writes, however, like a man thoroughly at home in the whole debate; to whom the vast range both of Oriental and Occidental learning is familiar. He meets the views of his opponent on the testimony of the African Church, and likewise his reasoning on the French and Waldensian versions, in the most triumphant manner, leaving not the shadow of argument unanswered. The reasonings for the authenticity of the prologue to the Catholic Epistles, on which so much stress has been laid, he also very ably refutes. In his third letter he brings forward a new translation of the genuine text, which he endeavors to defend and illustrate. Mr. Oxlee, like many other ingenious and able men, succeeds better in overthrowing the system of others than in sustaining his own. On a passage, however, which involves so many difficulties, and which is of hard interpretation, independently of what may be regarded as the true reading, it becomes us to be modest, whether in objecting to the views of others or maintaining our own. I am sorry I cannot give Mr. Oxlee's arguments in support of his new translation at full length; but it is due to him to give the principal passage.

"The connection of what is now the *eighth*, with the *sixth* verse, is so close that there is no understanding their import without furnishing the whole context. This I shall do, according to the *Alexandrine Manuscript*, which is supported in its reading of the sixth verse, not only by Cyrillus Alexandrinus, but by the later Syriac, the Armenian, the Coptic, and the Æthiopic versions. It is here given with the amended translation subjoined. Οὗτός ἐστιν ὁ ἐλθὼν διὰ ὕδατος καὶ αἵματος καὶ πνεύματος, Ἰησοῦς Χριστός· οὐκ ἐν τῷ ὕδατι μόνον, ἀλλὰ ἐν τῷ ὕδατι καὶ ἐν τῷ πνεύματι· καὶ τὸ πνεῦμά ἐστι τὸ μαρτυροῦν, ὅτι τὸ πνεῦμά ἐστιν ἡ ἀλήθεια. Ὅτι τρεῖς εἰσιν οἱ μαρτυροῦντες, τὸ πνεῦμα, καὶ τὸ ὕδωρ, καὶ τὸ αἷμα· καὶ οἱ τρεῖς εἰς τὸ ἕν εἰσιν.—'This is he who came by water, and blood, and spirit, Jesus Christ; not with the water only, but with the water and with the spirit: and the spirit is that which beareth witness; for the spirit is the truth. For there are three who attest or bear witness, the spirit, and the water, and the blood; and the three are for one thing.' The Armenian version of the sixth verse is as follows:—'This is he who came with water, and with spirit, and with blood, Jesus Christ; not with water only; but with blood and water: and the spirit is that which beareth witness; for the spirit is truth.' The Coptic reads thus:—'This is he who came by water, and blood, and spirit, Jesus the Christ: not with the water alone, but with the water and the blood; and the spirit beareth witness, for

H

the spirit is the truth.' The Philoxenian, or later Syriac version, as edited by Professor White, agrees with the Coptic. The Æthiopic version of this verse, in its present corrupt state, is evidently ungrammatical, and in the London Polyglot very inaccurately translated; but by omitting the prefix, *Beth*, before the repetition of the term, *Manfes*, Spirit, it will then, with the context, yield the following grammatical and consistent sense:—'And who is he that overcometh the world, except him who believes that the Lord Jesus is the Son of God; *Wacama, and that* he came by water, and by spirit, and by blood, Jesus Christ; and not by water only, but by water and by blood; and it is the spirit which beareth witness.'—That St. Cyrill, in the place above alleged, read the verse as it now stands in the Alexandrine Manuscript, is demonstrable from this circumstance, that, though he is made to cite it first as it stands in the generality of the modern Greek manuscripts; yet he soon after subjoins, Ἀλλὰ καὶ ἐν αἵματι καὶ ἐν πνεύματι; *But, also, with blood, and with spirit;* which is intelligible only on the supposition, that he had in the verse all the three terms, water, blood, and spirit, as they appear in that manuscript. It deserves to be remarked, too, that in the text of the Witnesses, instead of Ὅτι τρεῖς εἰσιν οἱ μαρτυροῦντες, *For there are three who bear witness*; he has, Ὅτι τρεῖς μαρτυροῦσι, *For three bear witness;* which, on being compared with the Latin version of the same verse, *Quia tres testimonium perhibent*, in the tract, *De Baptismo Hæreticorum;* warrants the conclusion, that, in some of the best Greek manuscripts of those early times, this reading was prevalent which we now find in St. Cyrill. So far as concerns the New Translation, it is perfectly immaterial which of the two readings should be preferred." *

The critical, grammatical, and theological objections to

* Oxlee's Letters, pp. 86–88.

this version, Mr. Oxlee endeavors to meet. With what success must be left to the judgment of the reader of his pamphlet.

The learned author of this reply to Mr. Nolan possesses very considerable acquaintance with several of the Oriental languages. It is evident both from this pamphlet, and from his "Three Letters to the Archbishop of Cashel, respecting his Grace's Apocryphal Publications," that he has a profound knowledge of the Rabbinical writings. He is also well acquainted with the Armenian version, which is rather an uncommon attainment in this country. The following passage contains valuable information respecting the reading in 1 John v. 7 of the MSS. of this version, and its present state.

"There is no trace of it in the Armenian version, which, as we now have it handed down to us, was made from Greek manuscripts of the Origenian or Eusebian recension at Constantinople, about the year 432, during the episcopate, and with the liberal assistance of the Constantinopolitan patriarch, Maximianus. In the first edition, indeed, of the Armenian Scriptures by Uscan, printed at Amsterdam in 1666, the text of the Heavenly Witnesses is inserted; but for this, as well as many other passages, Uscan has been severely handled by succeeding editors; as having attempted to corrupt the text from the Latin Vulgate, contrary to the authority of the Armenian manuscripts. In the edition of the New Testament printed at Venice in 1789, both the Earthly and the Heavenly Witnesses are included in a parenthesis; with the annotation in the margin, *That thus much is otherwise in the manuscripts.* Then, again, at the end of the volume, in their Advertisement to the reader, where they take occasion to explain their use of the parenthesis, the editors further inform us that, in respect of the passage under dispute, all their manuscripts, above ten in number, in conformity with the old Greek text, as well as with the Syriac and Arabic versions, exhibit the text in this short form. *Because the Spirit indeed is truth. These three there are who bear testimony, the spirit, and the water, and the blood; and the three are one. If we admit the testimony,* &c. That what was thus wanted in the great majority of the manuscripts, and without any tendency to illustrate the context, they had included within a parenthesis, as wholly obstructing the sense of St. John. In the critical edition, however, of the whole Bible printed at Venice in 1805, the spurious passage is wholly omitted; and the text restored, as above, according to the reading of the manuscripts. Since very few of my countrymen can boast of possessing this edition of the Armenian Scriptures, and still fewer, perhaps, of the ability to read it, I shall be doing probably an acceptable service to the English scholar, if I translate the whole annotation of the editors on the place, which is as follows: — 'Here, as well as in many other places, Uscan hath interpolated and altered the Armenian text from the Latin version, in this manner. *Who testifieth that Christ is truth. For there are three who bear witness in heaven, the Father, the Word, and the Holy Ghost; and these three are one. And there are three which bear witness on earth, spirit, water, and blood; and the three are one. If we admit the testimony of men,* &c. But out of about eighteen manuscript copies that we have, ancient as well as modern, not to mention two commentaries of universal reception, one alone, which was transcribed in the year 1656, about ten years before the printed edition of Uscan, exhibits the text in this form. *For the Spirit indeed is the truth. These are the three who testify in heaven, the Father, the Word, and the Holy Ghost; and these three are one. And there are three which testify on earth, the spirit, the water, and the blood. If we admit the testimony of men,* &c. Though there was also another manuscript copy, which on the surface had an equal and similar reading with this; yet the original or first reading had evidently been erased, and the intermediate space thus exactly filled up in smaller characters by a more recent scribe. But all the rest of our manuscripts, of whatever description, equally, and in accordance with a multitude of the more ancient Greek manuscripts, uniformly exhibit the text according to what we have found it our duty to give in the foregoing place.' — Thus in the beginning of the nineteenth century, the Armenians have happily rescued the printed text of their Scriptures from this audacious and manifest corruption of the language of St. John; and I have little doubt, that, could the authorized English version be again duly revised, the falsified text of which we complain would experience the same fate. In the interim, it is the duty of the clergy of the Church of England not to be more culpably negligent than others in vindicating the purity of the Holy Scriptures; and, if they cannot immediately remove from their version the spurious passage, at least not to be afraid to give publicity to the fraud." *

To few writers of the present age is the theological and critical reader more indebted than to the Rev. Dr. Hales, of Trinity College, Dublin. His "New Analysis of Chronology," which appeared in 1811 and following years, contains an immense mass of most valuable learning, not merely relating to chronology, but to all matters of a biblical nature. In the second volume of this work, pp. 905, 906, he has given his opinion, that the verse in question is spurious. Six years after this, however, Dr. Hales declared himself "at length perfectly satisfied of the authenticity and credibility of the disputed clause, from a more critical view of the whole of the evidence, *external* and *internal*, *for* and *against* it."

* Pp. 130 - 132.

The work in which this second opinion is avowed is his "Faith in the Holy Trinity, the Doctrine of the Gospel," &c. London, 1818. 2 vols. 8vo. Second thoughts are sometimes best, and the learned Doctor had an undoubted right to change his mind, on obtaining another view of the evidence from what he formerly had. But I cannot help expressing my surprise that a man of the cool and accurate mind of Dr Hales should avow so strongly his entire satisfaction of the authenticity of the passage, without being able to place the evidence on which that opinion is founded more satisfactorily before his readers.

In the second volume of this learned work on the Trinity (for learned it is, though I cannot assent to various parts of it,) there is a dissertation of one hundred pages on the disputed verse. In the course of the discussion contained in it, Dr. Hales travels over a great part of the ground without saying anything new, or placing the old argument in a more forcible light. He also commits some very considerable mistakes in parts of his statement. Speaking of Griesbach's account of the Greek MSS. of the New Testament, he says: —

"Deducting several manuscripts that are either mutilated or imperfect in this place, he counts 146 that omit the clause, as collated either by himself, or by others; namely, Simon, Wetstein, Matthäi, Blanchini, Birch, Lamy, Porson, Marsh, Clarke, Goldhagen, Sinner, and Travis; and he thus closes the account:

"'I may venture to assert confidently, that *there is no Greek manuscript, extant in Europe, in which the seventh verse is read.* For if such was anywhere found, a treasure so rare and desirable would have been brought to light long ago.'

"But of these 146 manuscripts, there are no more than

two of the oldest class, namely, the Alexandrine A, and the Vatican B, that omit the clause; for the Ephrem C is mutilated in this place, and the Cambridge D, the Laudian E, and Coislinian F, do not contain the Catholic Epistles. The rest are comparatively modern; none, probably, older than the ninth century, and many of much later date.

"The entire number of manuscripts, wholly or partly collated hitherto, does not much exceed 400; and these bear but a small proportion to those that have not been collated in the several libraries of Europe. There are many manuscripts in *uncial* letters, in the different libraries of Italy, which have never been collated. Of the numbers in the Vatican Library, only thirty-four have been collated. And since the death of Asseman, the celebrated Orientalist and Librarian of the Vatican, the difficulty of access to the manuscripts is so great as to make it almost impossible for a critic to derive, at present, any advantage from them. It is strictly forbidden, not only to copy, but even to collate them. In the year 1783, the Abbé Spoletti presented a memorial to the Pope, requesting permission to print the whole of the celebrated *Codex Vaticanus.* He was referred, according to the usual routine, to the Inquisition; whose permission was refused, under the plea, that 'the *Codex Vaticanus* differed from the *Vulgate,* and might, therefore, if *made known to the public,* be prejudicial to the interests of the Christian religion.'

"In the Florence Library alone are at least *a thousand* Greek manuscripts of the New Testament, two of which are of the Apocalypse; of these only twenty-four have been collated.

"In the Royal Library of Paris are 202 manuscripts, of which only 49 have been collated. See Marsh's Notes to Michaelis, Vol. II. pp. 642 – 647.

"Griesbach, therefore, has hazarded an unguarded and unfounded assertion, even with respect to the libraries of Europe. And how many ancient and valuable manuscripts may lie buried in the libraries of Constantinople, it is impossible to judge. That there are many, indeed, appears from the accounts given by the Abbé Toderini, in his Letteratura Turchesca, published at Venice in 1787, in 3 vols. 8vo. The Pope and the Mufti are equally adverse to the publication of hidden 'treasure so rare and so desirable' to the *Christian* world." *

Passing over other mistakes in this passage, there is one so perfectly absurd, that it is surprising Dr. Hales should not have perceived it. He gravely asserts, that "in the Florence Library alone there are at least a thousand manuscripts of the New Testament." And he as gravely refers to Michaelis for this fact. It is surprising it did not occur to Dr. Hales, that it is not generally believed that there are a thousand manuscripts of the Greek Testament in existence in all the world. The truth is, Michaelis, in the passage referred to, is speaking of Greek manuscripts in general, which Dr. Hales, by an unfortunate mistake, applies to the New Testament in particular. The whole of his hypothetical argument, therefore, is at once swept away. Instead of there being many uncollated manuscripts, there is reason to believe that there are comparatively few which have not been examined for evidence on this very passage; and all, with the exceptions that are so well known, and so little regarded, are against it.

Towards the conclusion of his dissertation, he expresses his confidence, that "it will be found exhaustive of the subject, and set the controversy at rest in future." † In this the learned Doctor has already found himself to be mistaken. The controversy still goes on, and must continue to do so,

* Vol. II. pp. 135 - 137.    † P. 225.

ll evidence is adduced of a very different kind, in favor of ıe verse, from what has ever yet been brought forward.

The next work I have to mention takes the opposite side om Dr. Hales, and is in all respects worthy of the critical arning and acumen of its author. His former labors on ıe subject have been already noticed. In the Sixth Part ? Dr. Marsh's (now Bishop of Peterborough) Course of heological Lectures, as Lady Margaret Professor of Diviny, which appeared in 1822, his Lordship again refers to this ›ntroversy, as affecting the credibility of the New Testament. [e shows, as I conceive, with considerable force of argument ıd ingenuity, "that if it be true in regard to the disputed ıssage, that the ancient Greek manuscripts, which have de:ended to the present age, with the works of the ancient ;reek fathers, and the manuscripts of the ancient versions, ıe oldest of the Latin version not excepted, have descended › us in a mutilated state, there is an end to that security hich is derived from their mutual agreement, for the integty of the New Testament in all other places. And we are rought at length into this dilemma: either to relinquish a art, or abandon the whole."

After noticing its absence from all the ancient Greek ıanuscripts and fathers, he thus endeavors to account for :s introduction. "At the *end* of the fourth century, the celbrated Latin father Augustin, who wrote ten treatises on he First Epistle of St. John, in all of which we seek in vain or the seventh verse of the fifth chapter, was induced, in ıis controversy with Maximin, to compose a gloss upon the ighth verse. Augustin gives it professedly as a gloss upon he words of the eighth verse, and shows, by his own reasonıg, that the seventh verse did not then exist. The high haracter of Augustin in the Latin Church soon gave celebrity to his gloss; and, in a short time, it was generally adopted. It appeared indeed under different forms; but it was still the gloss of Augustin, though variously modified. The gloss having once obtained credit in the Latin Church, the possessors of Latin manuscripts began to note it in the margin, by the side of the eighth verse. Hence the oldest of those Latin manuscripts which have the passage in the margin, have it in a different hand from that of the text. In later manuscripts we find margin and text in the same hand; for transcribers did not venture immediately to move it into the *body* of the text, though in some it is *interlined*, but interlined by a later hand. After the eighth century the insertion became general. For Latin manuscripts written *after* that period have generally, though not always, the passage in the body of the text. Further, when the seventh verse made its first appearance in the Latin manuscripts, it appeared in as many different forms as there were forms to the gloss upon the eighth verse. And though it now *precedes* the eighth verse, it *followed* the eighth verse at its first insertion, as a gloss would naturally follow the text upon which it was made. It is not, therefore, matter of mere conjecture, that the seventh verse originated in a Latin gloss upon the eighth verse: it is an historical fact, supported by evidence which cannot be resisted.

"But many centuries elapsed before the passage was exhibited in Greek. The first Greek writer who has given it is Manuel Calecas, who lived as late as the *fourteenth* century. And we need not wonder at finding the passage in *his* works, as Calecas was a convert to the Church of Rome. In the fifteenth century the passage was quoted by Bryennius, who was likewise so attached to the Church of Rome, that he quoted *other* readings of the Vulgate which are not found in the Greek manuscripts.

"At length, in the sixteenth century, a *Greek manuscript* of the New Testament appeared with 1 John v. 7. Its original appellation was Codex Britannicus: but it is now called the Dublin manuscript. It made its first appearance about the year 1520; and that the manuscript had just been written when it first appeared is highly probable, because it appeared at a critical juncture, and its appearance answered a particular purpose. But whether written for the occasion or not, it could not have been written *very long* before the sixteenth century. For this manuscript has the Latin chapters, though the κεφαλαια of Eusebius are likewise noted. Now the *Latin* chapters were foreign to the usage of the *Greek* Church, before the introduction of printed editions, in which the Latin chapters were adopted, as well for the Greek as for the Latin Testament.

"...... The Dublin manuscript, therefore, if not written for the purpose to which it was applied in the third edition of Erasmus, could hardly have been written more than fifty years before. And how widely those critics have erred in their conjectures, who have supposed that it was written so early as the twelfth century, appears from the fact, that the Latin chapters were not *invented* till the thirteenth century.

"But the influence of the Church of Rome in the composition of the Dublin manuscript is most conspicuous in the *text* of that manuscript, which is a servile imitation of the Latin Vulgate. It will be sufficient to mention how it follows the Vulgate at the place in question. It not only agrees with the Vulgate in the insertion of the seventh verse: it follows the Vulgate also at the end of the sixth verse, having χριστός, where all other Greek manuscripts have πνεῦμα: and in the eighth verse it omits the final clause, which had *never* been omitted in the Greek manuscripts, and was not omitted even in the *Latin* manuscripts before the thirteenth century.

Such is the character of that solitary manuscript, which is opposed to the united evidence of all former manuscripts, including the Codex Vaticanus and the Codex Alexandrinus." *

A singular work, in which this controversy is introduced, appeared in 1822, under the technical title of "Palæoromaica: or Historical and Philological Disquisitions: inquiring whether the Hellenistic style is not Latin-Greek? whether the many new words in the Elzevir Greek Testament are not formed from the Latin? and whether the hypothesis, that the Greek Text of many MSS. of the New Testament is a translation or re-translation from the Latin, seems not to elucidate numerous passages: to account for the different Recensions: and to explain many Phenomena hitherto inexplicable to Biblical Critics?"

The author of this volume, who was long concealed, and is not yet, I believe, generally known, was the Rev. John Black, Minister of Coylton, in the South of Scotland, and Author of the Life and Translation of Tasso. It would scarcely be supposed that the clergyman of a small and obscure parish north of the Tweed would be the author of a work which has troubled both the Universities of England. But the translator of Tasso was no ordinary man both in genius and learning.

In this singular volume, the author endeavors to revive something like the wild and exploded hypothesis of the Jesuit Hardouin, who maintained that our Lord and his Apostles spoke Latin, and that the Latin Vulgate was the original of the New Testament. The anonymous author of the Palæoromaica contends, that the Greek New Testament is a translation of a Latin original, the text of which is not preserved in the Vulgate, or any Latin version in being. He also

* Lect. XXVII. pp. 16-26.

maintains that it is a translation by an unknown writer, imperfectly acquainted both with Latin and Greek.

The proofs of these fanciful and extravagant notions, the reader will easily suppose, must be very extraordinary. The writer is by no means deficient in ingenuity, and has evidently spared no pains to bolster up his theory. He argues from the existence of certain analogous cases of translation from the Latin, and particularly from the Aldine edition of the Greek Simplicius: from the fact that, in the days of the Apostles, Latin, not Greek, was the prevailing language of Judæa, and other parts adjacent: and from the existence of numerous Latinisms, which, he thinks, he has discovered in the New Testament. But it may be proper to give his own analysis of his work.

"It consists," he says, "of six Disquisitions, in the first of which he examines the opinion, that a knowledge of Greek was general and almost universal in the age of the Apostles; an opinion which is, perhaps, proved to be at once contrary to probability, and contradictory to facts. In the second and third Disquisitions it is submitted, that, considering that at least one of the Gospels, and several of Paul's Epistles, were addressed to Latins, it might have been expected that such portions of the New Testament should have been sent to them rather in Latin than in Greek. Whatever was the primitive language, however, in which the Books of the New Testament were originally composed, and admitting that it was Greek, it is shown by numerous phenomena that at least our Elzevir text, or its basis, and, indeed, that of several other copies of the Greek Testament in the author's possession, (none of them, however, so old as our received English version,) bear marks of being a version from the Latin. It is submitted, that it seems not improbable that a translated or re-translated text may (as in Matthew's Gospel and various other remarkable instances which are exhibited) have supplanted the original; and that the Elzevir Testament may, like the *Aldine Simplicius*, be a Greek re-translation from the Latin of an original Greek work. This the author proceeds to corroborate, in the fourth Disquisition, by a list of words, phrases, &c., arranged into twelve different classes, all (if he mistakes not) tending to establish that what is named the *Hellenistic* style is not Hebrew, but Latin-Greek; and all seeming to support the conclusion, that the peculiarities of words and style in our Elzevir or Greek Vulgate are to be derived from a Latin original. In this Disquisition the origin of whole cohorts of Roman-Greek words, which have been singly the subjects of long dissertations, will be shown; and many of them which have frightened philologists by their portentous shapes, will be recognized as old acquaintances, somewhat mutilated and disguised.

"The author, in the fifth Disquisition, after attempting a solution of some apparent objections to or difficulties in his hypothesis, proceeds to show how much it seems to be supported by the sentiments and statements of some of the most distinguished Editors of the New Testament. It will be found that of these some have proceeded on the assumption that even the Latin Vulgate (itself a version from the Greek) is of greater authority than the modern Greek text; while others accuse the most venerable Greek MSS. of the New Testament, and, indeed, in proportion to their antiquity, of Latinizing. In the sixth and last Disquisition, the author applies his hypothesis to an elucidation of the German theory of different families or recensions of the MSS. of the New Testament; and here, as all along, he illustrates (if he mistakes not) numerous passages, and many various readings, which have hitherto resisted the efforts of all critics to explain them." *

* Preface, pp. viii.–xi.

On these grounds chiefly he raises his visionary structure, which, if true, would go far to endanger the whole fabric of Christianity. His learning is evidently considerable, but his love of paradox would seem to be still greater. The work was regarded, on its first appearance, as dangerous, and immediately occasioned a considerable controversy.

In the British Critic for January, February, and April, [1823,] a long and able article combated the main positions of the Palæoromaica. In the course of the same year, it was attacked by Bishop Burgess, in the Postscript to his Vindication of 1 John v. 7; by the Rev. J. T. Conybeare, in his "Examination of certain Arguments in Palæoromaica"; by Dr. Falconer, in the "Second Part of the Case of Eusebius"; and by the Rev. W. G. Broughton, in his "Examination of the Hypothesis advanced in a recent Publication, entitled Palæoromaica."

The last is the ablest and fullest exposure of the fallacy and absurdity of the whole scheme. The author, however, far from being discouraged by the number and weight of his opponents, again took the field against them all, in a "Supplement to Palæoromaica, with Remarks on the Strictures made on that Work by the Bishop of St. David's, the Rev. J. T. Conybeare, the British Critic; also by the Rev. W. G. Broughton, and Dr. Falconer." 1824.

To the second "Postscript" in this publication, Mr. Broughton replied in 1825. And the whole subject was again brought into review by Dr. Maltby, in a visitation sermon, entitled, "The Original Greek of the New Testament asserted and vindicated." Such is the present state of the Palæoromaican Controversy. It is very curious as a display of ingenuity, and as affording another proof that the text of the New Testament is capable of bearing any ordeal to which it is possible for the learning or genius of man to put it.

Having noticed the work itself, and the discussion which it occasioned, I must state how it came to be connected with the dispute about the Heavenly Witnesses. The author considers the disputed verse a specimen of translation from Latin, and therefore one of the supports of his argument for the Latin origin of the New Testament. The following passage contains the substance of his theory on this part of his subject.

"A still more appropriate example of the origin of recensions, arising from a diversity of versions from the Latin, may be given from an interpolation in the Greek New Testament itself. In his two first editions of the New Testament, Erasmus omitted the famous verse, 1 John v. 7, concerning the three heavenly witnesses, but inserted it in his later editions on the authority of a *Codex Britannicus.* This *Cod. Brit.* is supposed to be the *Cod. Montfortianus* or *Dublinensis,* one proof of which is, that the text of the third edition of Erasmus, printed in 1522, agrees *verbatim* in this interpolated passage with the Dublin MS., while it differs from all other editions, except such as wére copied from itself. Nor does it differ only from the usual text, but (as Michaelis observes) 'is written in such Greek as manifestly betrays a translation from the Latin.' I shall transcribe the interpolated words as they exist in the three celebrated editions of the New Testament.

"*Cod. Montfort. and Edit. Erasmi tertia, anni* 1522.

"*εν τῳ ὀυρανῳ, πατηρ, λογος, και πνευμα ἁγιον, και οὑτοι οἱ τρεις ἑν εισι. Και τρεις εισιν οἱ μαρτὺρουντες εν τη γη.*

"'Here (says Michaelis, ii. 286) the article is omitted before the words expressive of Father, Son, and Holy Ghost, because there is no article in the Latin, and it occurred not to the translator that the usual Greek was *ὁ πατηρ, ὁ λογος, το πνευμα.* He has also *εν τη γη*, which is false Greek for *επι της γης*, because he found in the Latin *in terrâ.*'

"*Editio Stephani tertia, anni* 1550.

"*εν τῳ ουρανῳ, ὁ πατηρ, ὁ λογος, και το ἁγιον πνευμα, και οὑτοι οἱ τρεις ἑν εισι. Και τρεις εισιν οἱ μαρτυρουντες εν τῃ γῃ.*

"Here Stephens, or rather, as Dr. Marsh observes, Erasmus himself, in his two last editions, has modelled the verse 'into better Greek by the insertion of the article.' Still, however, we have the Latinism *εν τῃ γῃ*. It has been proved irrefragably by several critics, that the Complutensian editors translated also the above verse from the Latin, and interpolated it into their Greek text. 'And it is no more than justice (says Porson) to allow that they at least did their work like workmen. They made good Greek of their Latin, — a task to which the translator of the Lateran Decrees, and the writer of the Dublin MS. were unequal.' This Complutensian text is as follows: —

"*Editio Complutensis, anni* 1514.

"*εν τῳ ουρανῳ, ὁ πατηρ, και ὁ λογος, και το πνευμα ἁγιον, και οἱ τρεις εις το ἑν εισι. Και τρεις εισιν οἱ μαρτυρουντες επι της γης.*

"In the above text, translated from Latin into Greek, we have a specimen of three different recensions arising from three different versions from the Latin; or, at least, from two immediate versions from that language, and an improvement upon one of them by modelling it into better Greek. This improvement is produced, in the first place, by an insertion of the articles. I formerly [p. 297] endeavored to account for the non-existence of the *dual number* in the Greek Scriptures, from the circumstance of its non-existence in the Latin, whence our Vulgate Greek copies may have been translated; and, in like manner, as the articles are wanting in the Latin language, there is usually a deficiency in this respect in every literal Greek version from the Latin. Thus, as we have seen above, we have in the Dublin MS., and in the edition of Erasmus, which was derived from it, *πατηρ* and *λογος* and *πνευμα* without any article. It is stated by Erasmus, in one of his Apologies, in speaking of his first edition, 'In calce *Apocalypsis* in exemplari, quod tum nobis erat *unicum*, nam is liber apud Græcos rarus est inventu, deerat *unus atque alter versus*. Eos nos addidimus secuti *Latinos* Codices.' Wetstein, who quotes this passage, remarks, 'Accuratius tamen omnia rimanti satis constat, non, ut Erasmus scribit, *perpauca* fuisse, quæ ipse ex Latinis utcunque et festinanter Græce reddidit, sed a vers. 16 ad finem libri sex integros versus. In istis enim omnibus Erasmi editio abit a Codicibus MSS., et ita quidem, ut Græca ipsius non obscurum sit ex Latinis fuisse conversa. Hinc enim profecta est perpetua illa omissio articulorum vers. 16, *ῥιζα* pro *ἡ ῥιζα*; *λαμπρος* pro *ὁ λαμπρος*; vers. 18, *προφητειας βιβλιου* pro *της προφητειας του βιβλιου*, *εν βιβλιῳ* pro *εν τῳ βιβλιῳ* bis; vers. 19, *βιβλου* pro *του βιβλιου*; *ζωης* pro *της ζωης*; *πολεως ἁγιας* pro *της πολεως της ἁγιας*.'"*

This, it must be confessed, is ingenious; but though it should be proved that the disputed passage was first translated into Greek by the Complutensian editors, or the writer of the Dublin manuscript, the argument of the Palæoromaica in favor of the Latin origin of the New Testament would by no means follow, as I suppose the disputed verse is the only passage in this particular situation. The author is aware of this, and therefore supports his hypothesis by other arguments, which it is no part of my business to answer. Those who wish to enter fully into this curious, and not uninteresting controversy, must consult the works on both sides which have been enumerated.

Having noticed several works in which the subject of this memoir is incidentally discussed, we come now to the latest stage of this important controversy, in which Dr. Burgess,

* Pp. 411 - 415.

formerly Bishop of St. David's, but now of Salisbury, makes the principal figure. 'Considering the learning and talents which had previously expended their resources and power on the merits of this question, a new aspirant to the honor of finally determining it might be expected to possess more than ordinary claims to the attention of the literary republic. Dr. Burgess was well known as a highly respectable clergyman; and as a prelate he was venerable for his years and his moderation. But his publications had been numerous rather than profound; neither distinguished by superior erudition, nor any particular traits of genius and originality.

In 1820, the Bishop published a volume of tracts on the Divinity of Christ, in which he expressed himself in favor of the disputed passage, and enters into a short argument in support of his opinion. But nothing in this tract requires particular notice.

In 1821, he commenced his labors in support of the testimony of the heavenly witnesses, by publishing "A Vindication of 1 John v. 7, from the Objections of M. Griesbach: in which a New View is given of the external Evidence, with Greek Authorities for the Authenticity of the Verse, not hitherto adduced in its Defence." In this pamphlet he endeavors to show that Griesbach's judgment on the text is precipitate, partial, contrary to his own rules of criticism, and untenable; — that Bengelius's conviction of its authority rested not on one argument, but on many; — and alleges that various reasons, which he assigns, may account for the loss of the verse in the ancient manuscripts. He argues that its absence from manuscripts now extant is no proof of its spuriousness, if it can be proved it was ever read in the most ancient Greek manuscripts. He maintains, on the authority of Cyprian, and the ancient Latin version, that this was the case. He argues both from the internal and external evidence in support of the common reading, and has evidently arrived at a very thorough conviction of its genuineness himself. Of Griesbach he says: —

"The substance of M. Griesbach's Diatribe consists of these positions: — that the controverted verse is not found in any Greek manuscript extant but one, and *that* a very recent manuscript of the fifteenth or sixteenth century; that it is not quoted by any of the Greek fathers; and that it rests chiefly, if not solely, on the authority of Vigilius Tapsensis. I have shown that he is mistaken in the last of these positions. He is also mistaken in the age of the Dublin manuscript, which Dr. Adam Clarke has shown to be a manuscript of the thirteenth century. If the verse has not yet been found in any other Greek manuscript, it may hereafter. The *Hymn to Ceres* had been lost for sixteen centuries, when it was discovered in a manuscript at Moscow, and that manuscript written as late as the end of the fourteenth century. If the verse is not quoted by any of the Greek fathers, it has been by two Latin fathers, who are more ancient than any Greek manuscript of the New Testament that is now extant." *

On the internal evidence of the verse he says: —

"Ernesti and Horsley were decided in their opinion of its authenticity by the internal evidence. And though Griesbach in his Diatribe on the verse dismisses this evidence, as I said before, hastily and contemptuously, yet he not only in his general rule for judging of the true reading of a passage gives the *first* place to the *interna bonitas* of the text, but on another occasion, in estimating the value of Codex Paulin. 17. in his Symbolæ Criticæ, he takes the internal evidence for his *chief guide*. Nay, in the Preface to his latest work, his Commentarius Criticus in Nov. Test. Part II., he repre

* Vindication, 2d edit., p. 99.

sents the use of MSS. and his distinction of recensions as of *very secondary* consideration, in comparison with the *interna veræ falsæve lectionis indicia.* I shall accordingly, in the following pages, reverse the method of inquiry into the authenticity of the verse which he observed in his Diatribe. I shall first consider the internal evidence, and then the external; and shall take a new view of its external history by dividing it into three periods: (1.) From the death of St. John to the end of the third century; (2.) From the beginning of the fourth century to the end of the ninth; (3.) From the beginning of the tenth to the date of the Complutensian, or first printed edition, in the sixteenth century; and shall apply to the two first periods two Greek authorities not hitherto adduced in defence of the verse."*

In speaking on the external evidence of the verse, to which the Bishop alleges Griesbach has done much injustice, he refers to two or three additional Greek evidences of great antiquity which he had to adduce. From this the reader might be led to expect the testimony of some newly discovered manuscripts, or the undoubted reading of some ancient Greek fathers. But no such thing: the Bishop has nothing of the kind to produce. His evidence is nothing but hypothetical argument and supposition, from beginning to end. In the first period of the Bishop's distribution no manuscripts whatever now exist. This absence of all evidence his Lordship converts into positive evidence in favor of the verse.

"In the view which we have taken of this first period, everything is favorable to the authenticity of the controverted verse. The *internal* evidence requires the verse; there is *no external evidence against it;* for there is no manuscript extant so ancient as this period; and we have good evidence

* Vindication, pp. 108, 109.

for it in the testimony of the Latin version of this period preserved by the African Church; beside the probability arising from the rejection of St. John's Epistles by the Alogi. These evidences cannot be invalidated by the absence of the verse from manuscripts of a *later period;* nor is it incumbent on the defenders of the verse to account for its *loss*, or for the *silence* of the Greek fathers; though the former may be accounted for from the homœoteleuton, if not from the mutilation of this very Epistle by those who wished to sever the humanity of Christ from his divinity; and the latter from the reasons given by Bengelius, and lately by Mr. Nolan, in his view of the subjects of religious controversy during the six first centuries." *

His reasoning respecting the second period is of the same novel and extraordinary character.

"In the second period of the external history of the verse, which comprehends six hundred years (A. D. 301 – 900), while the clear light of the internal evidence continues in all its force, the external evidence assumes a somewhat different character. In the former period there was no external evidence against the verse; in this there is some; but at the same time there is some for it: *negative* evidence against the verse, and *positive* for it. *All the Greek manuscripts extant* of this period omit the verse. But they are so few (not more than four) as to bear no proportion to the hundreds, perhaps thousands, that are lost, *many* of which might have contained it, as *some*, we know, did.

"There can hardly be a doubt that the seventh verse was extant in the Greek in the copies of Walafrid Strabo; and none at all of its existence in the time of the writer of the Prologue to the 'Canonical Epistles.' Walafrid Strabo, who lived in the ninth century, wrote a comment on the verse,

* Vindication, pp. 122, 123.

and the Prologue to the Epistles. He could not, therefore, be ignorant either of the *defects* which the author of the Prologue imputes to the Latin copies of his day, or of the *integrity* of the Greek, as asserted by him; and he directs his readers to correct the errors of the Latin by the Greek. The testimony of the Prologue is very material to *both* points." *

The Bishop's assertions respecting the Greek copies of Strabo, and the Prologue to the Epistles of John, are totally void of foundation, as both Porson and Marsh had successfully shown; yet on this untenable position the Bishop goes on to argue, that he "had arrived at *a certainty* that the controverted verse was extant in Greek manuscripts of the sixth or seventh century." He sums up in the following manner: —

"The authority of the African Church, as witnesses to the authenticity of 1 John v. 7, is not diminished by the allegories either of Augustin or his follower, Facundus. Nor is the validity of that testimony lessened by its being delivered in Latin instead of Greek. That the Latin Church was in possession of the Greek text, we know from Tertullian's appeal to the *literæ authenticæ* of the Apostles, (whether autographs or copies is of no consequence,) and the *authenticum Græcum* of St. Paul, in the second and third centuries; from the writer of the Prologue to the Epistles in the sixth or seventh century, and from Walafrid Strabo's references, in the ninth century, to the Greek text as the standard for correcting the imperfections of the Latin." †

It is deeply to be regretted that so respectable a person as the Bishop of St. David's should have undertaken a cause in which he so entirely fails; especially as he attaches so much importance to the question, and speaks so confidently

* Pp. 123, 124. † Pp. 139, 140.

of his success in establishing the claims of the passage. Reasoning more unsatisfactory has rarely ever been employed on a critical and theological subject; and both the evidence and the doctrines of revelation are affected by such a method of defending them.

The Bishop met with an opponent worthy of him and of the cause which he espoused, not in a Unitarian or a Dissenter, whom he appears to have considered the chief opponents of the verse, but in a learned member of his own church, and in a journal distinguished for its high-church principles and spirit. In the Quarterly Review for March, 1822, there appeared a very able article on the Bishop's pamphlet. In this critique his Lordship is treated with great courtesy and respect; but his evidence is entirely swept away, and his argument utterly demolished.

From the manner in which this article is written, arising necessarily from the nature of the work in which it appears, it is very difficult to separate the parts of the argument, so as to give any accurate view of the point and bearing of the whole. It glances at the controversy between Porson and Travis, notices the work of Nolan, and exposes some of its mistakes, objects to the mode of argument adopted, and sanctioned by Dr. Burgess, adverts to his attack on Griesbach, and to Middleton's objection, which we have already noticed. It then closes with the Bishop on the subject of the external evidence, and the new testimony which his Lordship adduces. After replying to several points, —

"The next authority appealed to is that of Cyprian, 'upon whom,' as Mr. Porson justly observed, 'the whole labor of supporting the verse is devolved.' In the treatise *De Unitate Ecclesiæ*, by that father, we read as follows: 'Dixit Dominus, Ego et Pater unum sumus; et iterum de Patre et

Filio et Spiritu Sancto scriptum est, Et hi tres unum sunt.' * This passage presents by far the strongest evidence that has been adduced in favor of the verse. The expression, 'scriptum est,' certainly implies that the words which follow, 'Et hi tres unum sunt,' were extant in Scripture; and, connected as they are with the mention of the three persons of the Trinity, the natural conclusion seems to be, that reference is made to the seventh verse of this chapter. Yet all who are conversant with the writings of the fathers must be well aware that their scriptural quotations are, for the most part, made from memory, and without that formal exactness which we now require. In the present instance, Cyprian may have had the above-cited passage of his master Tertullian in his mind, especially as he uses Filius (as Tertullian did) and not Verbum; he may therefore easily have confounded the 'qui tres unum sunt' of that passage with the 'hi tres unum sunt' of the eighth verse; under the impression that Tertullian interpreted the eighth verse of the Trinity. It is quite certain that Facundus conceived the passage in Cyprian to refer to the eighth verse. This, indeed, the Bishop of St. David's admits; but opposes to Facundus the authority of Fulgentius, who also quotes the same passage, and represents him as citing the seventh verse. Mr. Porson contends, that Fulgentius, by his own confession, became acquainted with the seventh verse solely by the means of Cyprian; but we are far from being convinced by the learned professor's arguments on this subject. In our opinion, which yet may be plausibly disputed, the legitimate inference from the words of Fulgentius is, that he had the verse in his copy of the Latin version. It does not, however, follow that he was

* [That is: — "The Lord has said, *I and the Father are one;* and again it is written concerning the Father and Son and Holy Spirit, *And these three are one.*" — Ed.]

correct in supposing that Cyprian quoted the seventh verse. We have stated the difficulty attending the passage in Cyprian; and the question for the reader's consideration is, whether the evidence which it supplies on the side of the verse be so weighty as to overbalance the great mass of evidence in the opposite scale." *

This, the Bishop will admit, is candid. It concedes there is difficulty respecting Cyprian; but after all, it leaves the matter in great doubt whether Cyprian really refers to the passage. It is perfectly absurd to found the authority of an important sentence of the word of God on such a basis. In reference to the novel part of the Bishop's argument, the following passage in the article is quite conclusive: —

"We now proceed to consider the Right Reverend author's *new* Greek authorities, of which, however, the first had been noticed by Mr. Nolan (p. 568), viz. 'the rejection of the writings of St. John by certain heretics of this (i. e. the first) period, whom Epiphanius calls ALOGI, on account of their denial of the Apostle's doctrine of the divinity of the Logos, or the Word.' Lardner has denied the existence of any heretics so called. But Lardner, it may be thought, was biassed by his peculiar opinions. Let us, therefore, grant that such heretics did exist, and that they rejected the First Epistle of St. John. Does it follow, as a necessary consequence, that 1 John v. 7 is genuine? Is not the very first verse of the Epistle sufficient to account for the rejection? Mr. Nolan, at least (p. 569), thinks that it is even more strongly opposed to the peculiar tenets of the Alogi than the disputed verse.

"With respect to the other Greek authority produced by the Bishop of St. David's, from the Pseudo-Clemens Alexandrinus, which he connects with a passage in Tertullian, we

* Quarterly Review, Vol. XXVI. pp. 332, 333.

can scarcely persuade ourselves that the learned prelate places any confidence in such a witness to the genuineness of the text in question. In return, however, for this 'authority,' we will present the Bishop and our readers with a short extract from a work printed in Potter's edition of Clemens. The work is entitled *Adumbrationes;* and is supposed by learned men to be a translation, by Cassiodorus, of some Commentaries on the Catholic Epistles, by Clemens Alexandrinus. 'Iste est, inquit, qui venit per aquam et sanguinem; et iterum, quia tres sunt qui testificantur; spiritus, quod est vita; et aqua, quod est regeneratio ac fides; et sanguis, quod est cognitio: et hi tres unum sunt. In Salvatore quippe istæ sunt virtutes salutiferæ, et vita ipsa in ipso filio ejus existit.' We do not ascribe any great weight to this extract, because there is much uncertainty respecting both the author and the translator of the work from which it was taken. Our principal reasons for adducing it are, that the testimony of Cassiodorus (to whom the translation is attributed) has been urged in defence of the 7th verse; and that the extract affords a singular confirmation of Mr. Porson's conjecture with regard to the reading which Cassiodorus found in his copy of St. John's Epistle. — *Letters to Travis*, p. 351.

"On the whole, it appears that the external evidence in favor of the verse, during the Bishop's first period, is reduced to the authority of Cyprian. Still, however, the learned prelate thinks that there is cause to triumph, inasmuch as the same period exhibits no evidence *against* the verse. What evidence of this kind can be required? It is admitted on all hands that there is no Greek MS. extant, so old as this period: but we have two MSS. of the fourth century, which omit the verse; and may we not justly infer that the MSS. from which they were copied omitted it also? Again, the verse has not been quoted by any of the Greek fathers of the second and third centuries. Does not this fact alone furnish strong presumptive evidence that during those periods it was not in existence? Can it be expected that passages should be produced from their writings expressly affirming the spuriousness of the verse, that is, the spuriousness of a verse, of the existence of which they were utterly ignorant?" *

No part of the discussion on this important subject has been more strenuously contended for on the one hand, or more resolutely resisted on the other, than the alleged authority of *Strabo*, in the *Glossa Ordinaria*, which Archdeacon Travis and Dr. Burgess maintain was written in the ninth century, and which, it is alleged, furnishes unquestionable evidence of the authenticity of the text. After quoting a passage from Travis to this effect, the present writer thus proceeds: —

"It is well known to the learned in these matters, and may easily be ascertained by those who will take the trouble to inquire, that the title of Walafrid Strabo to be considered as the author of the Glossa Ordinaria is, to use Mr. Porson's phrase, 'exceedingly questionable'; and that still more 'questionable' is his right to the Commentary on the Prologue to the 'Canonical Epistles.' Our present intention, however, is to prove that Walafrid Strabo CERTAINLY WAS NOT the author of the sentence quoted in the preceding statement, — a sentence from which so many consequences are deduced. That sentence forms the conclusion of a short tract which is prefixed to the *Glossa Ordinaria*, and entitled 'Translatores Bibliæ.' Had Mr. Travis taken the precaution of reading the entire tract, he would have found that the writer, in his account of the Septuagint translation, quotes, as his authority, a person whom he calls 'Magister in Historiis.' This appel-

* Pp. 333, 334.

lation had been given to Petrus Comestor, who flourished in the latter part of the *twelfth* century, and wrote a history of the Bible under the title of *Historia Scholastica.* The tract in question, therefore, could not have been written by Walafrid Strabo, who lived in the *ninth* century. What now becomes of Mr. Travis's argument founded on the ancient Greek MSS. which had been examined with the most critical exactness by Walafrid Strabo?

"As much importance has, by several writers, been attached to the supposed testimony of Walafrid Strabo, we have taken some pains to ascertain the real author of the tract from which Mr. Travis drew his quotation. We have now before us an edition of the Vulgate Bible, with the Glossæ and the Exposition of Nicholas de Lyra, printed at Venice by Pagninus, in the year 1495. Prefixed to the work is letter addressed to Cardinal Francis Picolhomini, by Bernardinus Gadolus, Brixianus. In this letter Gadolus describes the great care and diligence which he had employed, at the request of Pagninus, in preparing the edition; and concludes with the following sentence: 'Conscripsi præterea, sive ex multis auctoribus et præcipue ex Hieronymo excerpsi, tractatulum de Libris Bibliæ Canonicis et non Canonicis; qui si tuæ reverendissimæ dominationis judicio, cui omnia subjicio, comprobatus fuerit, eum ad utilitatem legentium imprimi permittam; sin nimis (l. minus) cellula continebitur.' * Then follows the Tract alluded to in the letter, entitled *De Libris Canonicis et non Canonicis;* to which is subjoined the Tract entitled *Translatores Bibliæ*, which fur-

* [That is: — "I have also written, or rather I have extracted from many authors, and especially from Jerome, a small treatise concerning the canonical and uncanonical books of the Bible; and if this shall be approved by the judgment of your Most Reverend Lordship, to whom I submit everything, I will allow it to be printed for the benefit of readers; otherwise it shall be retained in my cell." — Ed.]

nished Mr. Travis with his quotation. If any of our readers will take the trouble of examining these two tracts, we are convinced that not one of them will hesitate in attributing them to the same pen. In both, the style of composition is precisely the same, and the same authorities are alluded to viz. Origen, Jerome, Magister in Historiis. We must, therefore, conclude that, instead of affording a proof of the critical attention of Walafrid Strabo in the ninth century, Mr Travis's quotation will be found to attest the editorial diligence of Bernardinus Gadolus at the close of the fifteenth."*

So much for Strabo, and the Glossa Ordinaria of the *ninth* century, which we apprehend have now received their quietus forever. It is very worthy of remark, how Divine Providence furnishes the means, not only of maintaining the authority of the true Scriptures, but of destroying the pretences of what is false and apocryphal. We shall quote one more short passage from this able article, before proceeding to the next stage in the controversy.

"Some persons may be disposed to ask, — if, on the one hand, the agreement of the existing Greek manuscripts in omitting the verse affords a presumptive proof that it was omitted in the earlier manuscripts from which they are transcribed; and so on, till we arrive at the autograph of St. John, — does not, on the other hand, the agreement of the great majority of the manuscripts of the Vulgate in exhibiting the verse equally imply that it existed in the earlier Latin manuscripts, and, consequently, in the original copy of the Latin version? To this question we will reply by simply stating the circumstances of the two cases; first with regard to the Greek, and then with regard to the Latin manuscripts. On the Greek manuscripts we adopt the language of Matthäi: — 'Præterea, bona fide testor, me in nullo codice hoc

* Pp. 336, 337.

loco *lituram* deprehendisse, nec hujus loci *ullum vestigium* animadvertisse, nec in marginibus codicum, nec in scholiis, nec in catenis; cum tamen ad manus mihi fuerint tres codices cum scholiis ineditis orthodoxorum Theologorum, et unus, cum catena novendecim nobilissimorum Ecclesiæ Græcæ Patrum, sæculo ix scriptus.' * (*Matthäi ad loc.*) On the Latin manuscripts we remark: — The more ancient of them omit the verse: those manuscripts in which it appears, represent it under very different forms; some having the seventh verse before the eighth, and some after. In some manuscripts the seventh verse is found only in the margin; and in a very large portion the concluding clause of the eighth verse (*et hi tres unum sunt*) is omitted. From this comparative view of the state of the Greek and Latin manuscripts, as to the controverted text, we leave our readers to draw their own conclusions. In our own judgment there is but one conclusion that can fairly be drawn." †

As an auxiliary to the cause which he so warmly espouses, Bishop Burgess published, in 1822, a small volume of Latin tracts, with the following title: "Adnotationes Millii auctæ et correctæ ex Prolegomenis suis, Wetstenii, Bengelii, et Sabaterii, ad I. Joan v. 7. Una cum duabis epistolis Richardi Bentleii et Observationibus Joannis Seldeni, C. M. Pfaffii, J. F. Buddei, et C. F. Schmidii de eodem loco," &c. As this is merely a collection of tracts written in support of the disputed passage long ago, containing no new argument, it requires no further notice. The Bishop's object is to show, that

* [That is: — "Moreover, I testify in good faith, that in no manuscript have I found any erasure in this place, nor have I discovered any vestige of the passage either in the margin of manuscripts, or in scholia, or in catenæ; though I have had at hand three manuscripts with unpublished scholia of orthodox theologians, and one, written in the ninth century, with a catena of nineteen of the noblest fathers of the Greek Church." — Ed.]

† Page 339.

all the learned, at least, have not abandoned the defence of the passage.

His Lordship produced, in 1823, a second edition of his Vindication, to which are added, "A Preface in reply to the Quarterly Review, and a Postscript in answer to a recent Publication, entitled, Palæoromaica." The preface is the only thing in this publication, beside an advertisement of forty-two pages, with which we have now to do. It consists of sixty-eight pages. In this the Bishop professes to meet the Quarterly Review; but in reality never closes with the main argument of the controversy. There is a great deal of petty skirmishing, — a large portion of dust raised; but little done to satisfy the objector, or to relieve the subject of the difficulties under which it labors. His Lordship still maintains, with a positiveness that is very extraordinary, — "That *while we have much positive evidence for the verse, there is* NO POSITIVE EVIDENCE AGAINST IT."*

It is strange, in the present advanced stage of biblical literature, that it should be asserted there is no positive evidence against a sentence purporting to belong to the Bible, which is to be found in no genuine manuscript, and unsupported by the ancient versions. Can his Lordship require to be informed, that the only positive evidence in support of a passage of Scripture is its existence in authentic copies? If this be departed from, on the ground that we admit one verse, we may admit a hundred; and thus the whole evidence and character of revelation might be changed. The Bishop still continues to reiterate and defend his two new authorities, and actually adduces some others. But they are all of the same questionable character; witnesses which do not admit of cross-examination. These authorities are Diodorus, according to Theodorus Anagnosta, and quoted by Suidas. Mark

* Page 15.

the roundabout way in which we are furnished with his testimony; and mark still further what it is. Why, this Diodorus, who it seems was the Preceptor of Chrysostom, wrote on the 1st Epistle of John, and on "Unity in the Trinity"; from which the Bishop infers 1 John v. 7 was in his Greek copy of the New Testament! There is really no arguing with this kind of evidence, even with the authority of Dorhout to bolster it up.

The Bishop has another new authority, Dionysius of Alexandria. But this is no better than the former. The disputed verse is not quoted by Dionysius, nor any argument founded upon it in his writings. If "remote conclusions may be thus drawn at a jump," there is scarcely anything, however destitute of foundation, which may not be proved or disproved.

In the conclusion of this preface, his Lordship recapitulates what he considers the substance of his argument, and the leading grounds on which the genuineness of the passage may be defended. The reader shall have the benefit of this statement in his own words.

"For myself, I adhere, with increased conviction of its authenticity, to the declaration which excited the Reviewer's 'astonishment'; founded on the following reasons, with which I recapitulate the substance of this preface:—

"1. The connection of the verse with the context, and with the general scope of the Epistle; which Bengelius says, *omnem codicum penuriam compensat* [makes amends for all the want of manuscripts].

"2. The evidence of the Latin Version, *Græcis omnibus codicibus antiquior* [more ancient than any Greek manuscript]. (Bengelius.)

"3. The testimony of Tertullian and Cyprian, which Mill says is abundantly sufficient to authenticate the seventh verse;

*licet in nullis omnino ab illo tempore in hunc usque diem exemplaribus comparuerit* [even if it has been found in no copies from that day to this].

"4. The testimony of Fulgentius, who places beyond all doubt Cyprian's *direct citation of the seventh verse.*

"5. The testimony of Eucherius and Cassiodorus, who quote *both verses.*

"6. The testimony of the African Bishops, *instar centenorum codicum, qui optimæ notæ sunt seculi V.* [equivalent to that of a hundred of the best MSS. of the fifth century]. (Dorhout.)

"7. The quotations or allusions of the Greek fathers, Clemens of Alexandria, Dionysius of Alexandria, Basil, Athanasius the younger, Diodorus, the preceptor of Chrysostom, Cyril of Alexandria, Maximus, and the Greek Scholia.

"8. The testimony of the Prologue of the Canonical Epistles to the Greek text of the 7th verse, extant in the time of the writer.

"To these positive reasons for the authenticity of the verse, we may add the following negative arguments.

"If there are no Greek manuscripts but one, *for* the verse, *after* the end of the third century, there are no Greek manuscripts *against* the verse *before* that time.

"If no *Greek fathers* quote the *Greek text*, (which cannot be admitted,) no *Latin heretics* object to the *Latin text.* The Greek Church objected to the insertion of *Filioque* in the Latin Creed, but never to the text of the seventh verse in the Latin version.

"If no Greek father quoted 1 John v. 7, no Greek father quoted 1 John v. 20 during the first three centuries, or 1 Tim. iii. 16 during the first four." *

* Burgess, pp. 66 – 68.

In further prosecution of what the Bishop appears to have made a considerable part of the business of his latter years, he published, in 1824, "A Selection of Tracts and Observations on 1 John v. 7." This, like his Latin collection, is a useful compilation. It consists of Bishop Barlow's letter to Mr. Hunt, now first published from a manuscript in the Queen's College Library, Oxford; Bishop Smalbroke's Letter to Dr. Bentley, with Dr. Bentley's Answer; Extracts from Martin's Examination of Emlyn's Answer relative to that Letter; the Notes of Hammond and Whitby on the controverted Verse; and Dr. Adam Clarke's Account of the Montfort Manuscript.

Though it is convenient to be furnished with all these tracts in one volume, they throw exceedingly little light upon the controversy. The testimony of one undoubted manuscript of the New Testament, or a correct quotation of the passage in any ancient Greek writer, would be worth a whole host of opinions of modern writers, however learned and ingenious.

Prefixed to these tracts are an introduction and preface of seventy-two pages, by the Bishop himself, in which various points in the controversy are adverted to, and some account given of the several tracts which are introduced; but in which I do not observe anything which calls for particular observation.

In the same cause, so warmly espoused by Dr. Burgess, two other combatants, on opposite sides, appeared about the same time. The first of these, Mr. Oxlee, of whom some notice has already been taken, produced "Three Letters, addressed to the Rev. Fred. Nolan, on his erroneous Criticisms and Mis-statements in the Christian Remembrancer, relative to the text of the Heavenly Witnesses; in which are contained, also, Strictures on the Vindication of the spurious Passage by the Bishop of St. David's: together with a new Translation of the genuine Text, proposed and defended from every cavil," 1825.

The other, under the fictitious signature of Ben David, addresses "Three Letters to the Editor of the Quarterly Review, in which is demonstrated the Genuineness of the Three Heavenly Witnesses," 1825.

To Mr. Oxlee's remarks on Mr. Nolan we have already adverted, in noticing the work of that able and ingenious writer. We have here only to do with his strictures on the Bishop of St. David's. We are sorry to say, that they are written in a tone and manner more resembling the spirit of Porson, than the temper which always distinguishes Dr. Burgess in his controversial works. Mr. Oxlee, in his second letter, endeavors to refute the arguments adduced by Mr. Nolan and Dr. Burgess for the authenticity of Jerome's Prologue to the Catholic Epistles: and in the third letter he introduces what he considers a clear and connected view of the text and its context. His amended translation has been already given, with some of his remarks in its support. It is due to Mr. Oxlee, perhaps, to give another extract from his ingenious pamphlet, in which he supports his views of the reading of the text, by arguments derived from the connection.

"To me the immediate connection of the three witnesses with the sixth verse appears to have originated from a natural association of ideas in the mind of the holy Apostle. Having asserted that the Spirit giveth testimony, because it is the truth; he quickly calls to mind, that, as the Holy Spirit bearing witness within us, is the truth; so also are the Word, or the Son, and the Father, the truth; and so equally concurring witnesses with the Spirit itself, which proceeds from them both. The conjunction ὅτι, therefore, as Grotius has well observed on this text, has not so much a causative as a continuative and argumentative signification; and consequently, as well here as in other places of the Syriac version, it is rendered by the simple copulative: and in the Armenian Version is wholly omitted. The connection of the sense is as though he had said, — Nay, there are even three, the Father, the Word, or the Son, as well as the Spirit, who are attesting witnesses of the water, the blood, and the spirit, by which Christ came to erect his holy church; and these three are for one thing, that is, are accounted εἰς τὸ ἕν πνεῦμα, for one and the same Spirit; the same Evangelist having elsewhere declared, that *God is a Spirit.* If then we receive the testimony of men, such as John the Baptist, who testified of Christ, that he had descended from heaven, as the Son of God, to baptize with water and the Holy Ghost, — if, I say, we are willing to admit such human testimony as this; the testimony of the Father, and of the Son, and of the Holy Ghost, unto whose name every Christian man is baptized, and who dwell inseparably in the hearts of the faithful, is still greater and more to be depended on, in that they are the truth itself, and cannot possibly deceive us."

The pamphlet certainly abounds in very able and ingenious reasonings, and displays no small portion of literature; but it is offensively warm. There is little occasion for the *odium theologicum* in a discussion, which, it is now well understood, does not affect the doctrine of the Trinity, whichever side gains the ascendency. Criticism may be erroneous, and mistakes may be unintentionally made, but they ought to be opposed with calmness and firmness: and where men of so much eminence rank on different sides, a degree of modesty is more becoming than fierceness and dogmatic confidence. To Mr. Oxlee I shall have occasion to advert once more.

The author of Ben David, the late Dr. Jones, was a Socinian, and a man of considerable genius and learning, but fond of paradox. A defence of the disputed passage from such a quarter naturally suggests strong suspicions that there was something under it.

"Timeo Danaos dona ferentes."

His object is to prove that the disputed verse forms the subject of the whole Epistle, and that the true sense places its genuineness beyond all reasonable suspicion. In his first letter he endeavors to show that the object of the First Epistle of John was to check the Gnostic heresy, which maintained that the Creator is an evil, imperfect being, and that Christ was a God, either dwelling for a season in the man Jesus, or an empty phantom in his shape. The design of John, therefore, was to overthrow the divinity, and to assert the simple humanity of Christ!

In the second letter he gives what he conceives to be the scope and sense of the passage, "There are three bearing testimony in heaven, the Father, the Word, and the Holy Spirit; and these three are one."—"The meaning, then, is," he says, "that the Father, the Word, and the Holy Spirit, which are in heaven, bear testimony; and these three testimonies are one testimony; or, as it is expressed in the parallelism in the next verse, agree in one testimony. The testimony meant is that which it is the burden of the Epistle to prove, namely, that JESUS IS THE CHRIST; meaning, in opposition to the Antichristian teachers, that the man Jesus, and not a God dwelling in the man Jesus, or in the empty form of the man Jesus, is the Christ."

The object of the third letter is to prove the authenticity of the verse; in which, as might be expected, there is an entire failure. He acknowledges that he has no new evidence to adduce, and his hypothetical arguments and reasonings are unworthy of any attention. If Ben David wrote in jest, he deserves the severest reprobation; if in earnest, his folly deserves our pity.

Bishop Burgess published, in 1825, "A Letter to the Clergy of the Diocese of St. David's on a Passage of the Second Symbolum Antiochenum of the Fourth Century, as evidence of the Authenticity of 1 John v. 7." This creed was drawn up by a Council held at Antioch, consisting of ninety-seven bishops, of whom nearly half were Arians. After the declaration of faith in one God, our Lord Jesus, and in the Holy Ghost, the Creed adds, ὡς εἶναι τῇ μὲν ὑποστάσει τρία, τῇ δὲ συμφωνίᾳ ἕν. "So that they are three in person, and one in consent." There is, no doubt, some similarity between this passage and 1 John v. 7; but similarity and identity are very different things. It is as plain as possible that the words of the Creed are not a quotation from the disputed text. And although his Lordship argues that there is not a greater difference than sometimes obtains in the quotations made from the Old Testament in the New, we do not think he proves his point, as scarcely any of the words in the two passages are the same. Had the passage existed in the text of John at the time, it is too plain and too important not to have been quoted *verbatim et literatim*, instead of being only alluded to. I cannot perceive that the cause of the authenticity of the text gains anything from the Antiochian Creed.

In a large postscript, his Lordship endeavors to adduce evidence from the accounts given by Euthymius and Socrates of the origin of the Arian controversy, in support of his view of the question. The reasoning, however, of Porson on this subject, from page 119 to 226 of his letters, I do not conceive the Bishop has at all affected. It is not only not evident that Euthymius quotes the passage; but highly probable, as Porson shows, from another part of his works, that it did not exist in the MS. he used. "So far," says Porson, "therefore is Euthymius Zigabenus from having employed this weapon against the heretics, that, on the contrary, it is plain he never had it to employ. It was not to be found in the shops of those artificers of faith, who furnished him with the materials for his *Panoply*."

A considerable portion of the postscript is occupied with replying to Oxlee's Three Letters to Mr. Nolan. In this portion of his pamphlet his Lordship adduces another Greek authority, — a Greek MS. too. What a εὕρηκα would resound through the world if this document was forthcoming. But, alas! it is only something which was seen: when looked for again it was not to be found, — and is now gone. Such seems to be the fate of all the evidence of which the supporters of this passage boast. But hear the Bishop: —

"I must not here omit an important accession to the direct evidence for the verse, which I add on the authority of the present learned Rector of Lincoln College, in Oxford. Having heard it reported, that a Greek MS. of the New Testament containing the verse had been known to be extant in the library of Lincoln College, not many years since, and that the Rector of Lincoln had spoken of it in St. Mary's pulpit, I wrote to the learned Rector on the subject, and received the following answer: 'Porson's book never shook my conviction of the authenticity of the important verse, which has so long and laudably engaged your indefatigable study. The artful and superficial way in which he treated the interesting subject, and his unmannerly behavior to Mr. Travis, brought me some years ago into St. Mary's pulpit, with a sermon upon the disputed text; which sermon I have mislaid, and cannot find. What I said about the MS. that I had seen, which contained the verse, I cannot accurately state. It was a MS. in the College Library, and seen in the presence of Dr. Parsons, late Bishop of Peterborough; but on looking for it when I preached the sermon, it was not found, nor can it be found at the present time." *

When this manuscript is produced, it will be time enough to examine its character and pronounce on its pretensions.†

To the Bishop and Ben David the Quarterly replied in an able and very respectful article in their Sixty-fifth Number, for December, 1825. Here the learned Reviewer, after some introductory remarks, combats his Lordship's assertion after Travis, "that the verse was extant in the Greek in the copies of Walafrid Strabo," by showing that there is no evidence that Strabo understood Greek, or that he was the author of Glossa Ordinaria, or that he was the author of the Commentary on the Prologue to the Catholic Epistles, and that the Preface to the Glossa Ordinaria, in which he directs that the Latin MSS. should be corrected by the Greek, instead of being written by him, was written some centuries after his death. This is one of the Bishop's main positions, — at best it would not prove a great deal, but it really vanishes into smoke when touched by the finger of critical investigation. There are some good remarks in the article on the impropriety of preferring the Latin to the Greek fathers, a tendency which the views and classification of Griesbach has tended to produce. On the internal evidence which is supposed to be in favor of the verse, and the alleged grammatical difficulties of the passage, on the supposition of the seventh

* Burgess's Letter, pp. 84, 85.

† [Scrivener, in his Plain Introduction to the Criticism of the Text of the N. T., (1861,) p. 459, note, remarks: "There can be no question that he meant Act. 33, which does not give the verse, but has long been known to have some connection with the Codex Montfortianus, which *does*." See also the Vindication of Porson by *Crito Cantabrigiensis*, pp. 358, 359. — ED.]

verse being spurious, some good observations occur; particularly on a passage remarkably similar, from Gregory Nazianzen. The learned critic also offers some defence of Porson, in reply to several of the remarks of Dr. Burgess on that eminent scholar. The Bishop's Letter to the Clergy of St. David's is satisfactorily shown to contain nothing that will bear the test of close examination, or on which a defence of the passage can be rested. The notice of Ben David is little more than an intimation that he is not in earnest on the subject, and must have smiled on finding the Bishop of St. David's so much concerned to defend a passage no longer capable of support on sonnd critical principles. The whole discussion in the Quarterly Review is highly interesting. It is carried on very dispassionately, and with great force of argument. I regret that my limits will not allow me to quote several parts of the article; but the following passage, containing an answer to the Bishop's argument founded on the Symbolum Antiochenúm, deserves particular attention. The Bishop's argument has been already given; the reply is conclusive.

"In justice to the cause which the Bishop defends, we think it right to state, that, his Lordship having communicated the substance of his work to several of his right reverend brethren, the preceding argument appears to have had great weight with them. In letters from which we are favored with extracts, the Bishops of Winchester, Durham, and Hereford, together with other prelates, whose names are not mentioned, have expressed themselves either as almost, or as entirely, persuaded that the verse is genuine. With the sincerest respect for the learning and judgment of these eminent persons, we shall now venture to examine the argument. *They are three in person, and one in consent,* — savors much more of an illative distinction of the fourth century, than of a simple dictum of the apostolic age. Accordingly, the Bishop is obliged to omit 'the terms by which the quotation is disguised,' before he can imagine the expression to be derived from Scripture. And when the sentence has gone through this process, what remains? Not, as his Lordship states, *the three are one;* but *they are three indeed, but also one* (ὡς εἶναι τρία μὲν, ἓν δέ). Now, without being fastidious as to the gender of the numeral (τρεῖς or τρία), we affirm that this is *not* a quotation of 1 John v. 7 (οἱ τρεῖς ἕν εἰσι), — a sentence of a totally different form. But this is not all. The words SO THAT, which introduce the expression *they are three in person, and one in consent,* would lead us to suspect that the sentiment is an inference from some scriptural authority just preceding; whereas we are to suppose, from the Bishop's statement, that the avowal of a belief in the Father, the Son, and the Holy Spirit, is immediately followed by the expression, *so that they are three in person, and one in consent.* Let us therefore refer to the creed itself, as it appears in the translation given by his Lordship.

"'We believe in one God ..... and in one Lord Jesus Christ ..... and in the Holy Ghost, who is given to believers, for consolation, and sanctification, and perfection, according to our Lord Jesus Christ's direction to his disciples, saying, *Go ye unto all nations, baptizing them in the name of the Father, and the Son, and the Holy Ghost;* the Father being truly a Father, the Son truly a Son, and the Holy Ghost truly a Holy Ghost; the names being given not vainly and unmeaningly, but accurately expressing the respective subsistence (or person, ὑπόστασιν), order, and glory of each of those named (τῶν ὀνομαζομένων); SO THAT *they are three in subsistence* (or *person,* ὑποστάσει) *and one in consent.*' — (p. 104.)

"And thus it is as clear as words can make it, that the expression, *They are three in subsistence* (or *person*), *and one in consent*, is *not* a quotation of 1 John v. 7; but is derived, solely and entirely, from the baptismal commission in St. Matthew. We have seen many weak arguments in defence of the verse, but we trust his Lordship will excuse us if we frankly say, that an argument less effective than this it has never been our lot to meet with." *

From the ability and learning displayed in this last article of the Quarterly Review, in which the arguments of Bishop Burgess are most triumphantly met, it might have been anticipated that the Controversy was drawing to its close. But, alas, how vain human expectations frequently prove! The debate, judging from publications that have recently appeared, seems as far from a termination as ever. And, indeed, on the plan on which it is now conducted, it may go on forever. This memoir, therefore, is likely to close, while the warfare still rages. But as every important argument on each side has already been noticed, the review of the remaining publications will be as brief as possible.

From the conspicuous and decided part which Professor Porson took in this Controversy, his name has been more or less mixed up with all the discussions which have since taken place. One great object of Bishop Burgess, in his various publications, has been to diminish the general confidence of the literary republic, not in the scholarship of Porson, for that it would have been vain to touch, but in the accuracy of his acquaintance with biblical manuscripts, and the correctness of some of his data and reasonings in this celebrated Controversy. The Bishop charges that distinguished scholar with "mistakes," with unfounded opinions respecting the "genius of the Greek language," with making "disingenuous

* Quarterly Review, Dec. 1825, pp. 101, 102.

quotations," with "deficient knowledge of the Greek fathers," &c., &c.

It is not surprising, therefore, that among the friends, or disciples, or admirers of Porson, some one should step forward in his defence. It was due to his character, as a scholar of the first order, as a critic distinguished for his acuteness and his comprehension, and for the fearless honesty with which he avowed and defended his opinions, that his reputation should be vindicated from unmerited charges. He has met with a vindicator in all respects worthy of him, and of the cause which he has undertaken to defend, — one whom Porson himself would have been pleased to acknowledge as a friend and a coadjutor. I refer to the author of the following work: —

"A Vindication of the Literary Character of Professor Porson, from the Animadversions of the Right Rev. Thomas Burgess, D.D. F.R.S. F.A.S. P.R.S.L. Lord Bishop of Salisbury, in various Publications on 1 John v. 7. By Crito Cantabrigiensis. Cambridge, 1827." 8vo. Report ascribes this learned and able volume to the Rev. Dr. [Thomas] Turton, Regius Professor of Divinity in that University.* He who studies the articles in the Quarterly Review, and Crito Cantabrigiensis, will not, I apprehend, be very wide of the mark, if he ascribe both to the same individual. But the writer, be who he may, is of less importance than the book; though, certainly, he has no reason to be ashamed of this production of his pen.

The discussion is throughout conducted in the most gentlemanly and delicate manner. In his mode of carrying on the Controversy he has improved greatly upon Porson, as there scarcely ever occurs an expression calculated to wound or of-

* [Afterwards (1842) Dean of Westminster, and (1845) Bishop of Ely.— Ed.]

fend. He is calm and dignified; but firm and conclusive in all his reasonings. I regret that it is impossible to do any justice, even to the bare statement of his argument. The work is by no means restricted to a defence or vindication of Porson; on the contrary, it embraces the whole range of the Controversy, and discovers the author's familiarity with all its ramifications and details. The conclusion of the volume, in which Crito vindicates Porson's qualifications as a Scripture critic, is all I shall quote as an illustration of the style and manner of the author, rather than as a view of the contents of his book. Those qualifications are thus called in question by Bishop Burgess.

"The numbers in array against the verse are not so numerous as the advocates for it. No one country has entered so frequently and fully into this inquiry as our own. And (excepting living writers) who is there to oppose to the learning of Selden, Pearson, Hammond, Stillingfleet, Wallis, Bull, Mill, Waterland, and Horsley? I do not except Mr. Porson, when opposed to the great names before mentioned, *on such a subject as our present*, which does not admit the exercise of that peculiar sagacity which distinguished his conjectures on the text of the ancient Greek Poets, and the laws of Greek metre, and the peculiarities of Greek idiom; but requires other aids of learning, human and divine, in which Pearson and Bull had no superior. Mr. Porson, indeed, brought nothing new to this inquiry but what is, in a great degree, extraneous to it, — his wit, and humor, and dexterity in exposing the inaccuracy of his opponent. He has brought no objection to the passage, which had not been anticipated by Sir Isaac Newton, Whiston, Emlyn, or Dr. Benson." (*Vind.* p. 57.)

"When Mr. Boyle mentioned some eminent writers, whose sentiments he stated to be in accordance with his own, Dr.

Bentley replied, — that, 'if such were their opinion, yet it signified nothing, — for he went not by authorities but by truth. If they believed so, they were certainly mistaken.' We know, indeed, that scholars of high character have frequently judged erroneously of ancient works. 'What clumsy cheats,' as the same great critic remarks, 'those Sibylline Oracles, now extant, and Aristeas's story of the Septuagint, passed without control, even among very learned men.' Selden, the first writer on Bishop Burgess's list, founds an argument in Chronology upon the Letters of Phalaris, as if they had really been written by the Tyrant: — shall we, on that account, hesitate to reject them, as spurious productions? Pearson draws up a long and learned note to vindicate the orthodox reading of 1 Tim. iii. 16. After employing, on that occasion, principles of criticism which would overturn 1 John v. 7 in an instant, he quotes the latter incomparably more dubious text, without a word in its support: — can that be a reason why *we* should uphold it? — The learning of Hammond, Stillingfleet, Wallis, and Bull is readily acknowledged; but if any one will examine their observations on the controverted text, he will find that but a scanty portion of it has been brought to bear upon that point: — and what is their *authority* compared with the arguments of Mill and Bengelius? — Waterland is said to have become a convert to the opinion that the verse is genuine, in consequence of Twells's defence of it, — a story which, for the credit of Waterland, is, I hope, not true: — but what has Waterland produced in behalf of the verse? — Pearson and Bull, indeed, are the champions, whose very presence is deemed sufficient to put an end to contention; and I cannot but suspect that, while his Lordship is contemplating PORSON on one side of the question, and those great men on the other, a feeling gradually comes over him somewhat similar to that which prevailed at the Council of Trent, — a sort of horror at the idea that 'Grammarians should take upon them to teach Bishops and Divines.' *En rem indignam,* said the adversaries of Erasmus, — *Nos, qui jam tot annis sumus Doctores sacræ Theologiæ, denuo cogimur adire ludos literarios.**

"But, according to the learned prelate, an inquiry into the genuineness of this famous text 'does not *admit* the exercise of that peculiar sagacity which distinguished Mr. Porson' in other subjects. Now surely there is something very paradoxical in the notion, that sagacity, however refined, should form an obstacle, as it were, to success in any department of literature. If his Lordship had contented himself with saying that inquiries like the present do not *absolutely require* an extraordinary degree of sagacity, the truth of the position might, perhaps, have been allowed. Much, no doubt, that is deserving of attention, may be accomplished without it. But when we consider the expanse over which even a partial view of the subject has actually conducted us, and the dark and dreary regions through which we might have been led, we cannot, I think, but feel the advantages to be derived from a critical sagacity like that of Mr. Porson. The acuteness of his understanding was not confined to 'the laws of Greek metre and the peculiarities of Greek idiom'; and in researches into Ecclesiastical antiquity, — where there are works of dubious origin to be estimated, — where, in productions of which the authenticity is undoubted, there are obscure passages to be illustrated, and corrupt ones to be restored, — where, in fact, there are discrepancies of all kinds to be reconciled, — we may confidently assert that the leading qualities of Mr. Porson's mind were exactly those from which the world might have anticipated the happiest results.

* [That is: — "It is a shameful thing; we, who for so many years have been Doctors (or teachers) of sacred Theology, are again sent to school." — ED.]

"Pearson and Bull deserve all their fame for 'learning, human and divine'; but, as they never took a prominent part in defence of the verse, why should their acquirements be brought forward for the purpose of throwing those of Mr. Porson into the shade? The learned prelate has long been acquainted with the Letters to Travis; he has had the most ample means of discovering their vulnerable points; and he has finally selected those, I conclude, which he considered the most open to attack: — and yet I will venture to affirm, that, numerous as are the observations on which he has thought proper to animadvert, there is not one instance in which Mr. Porson appears deficient in learning, human or divine. Of the truth of this proposition the reader has now an opportunity to judge for himself.

"But Mr. Porson, it is alleged, advanced no new objection to the verse. — His purpose was to state the principal grounds of the controversy, and to examine Mr. Travis's arguments. He hinted, however, that if anything which had not been adduced should occur to him in the course of his investigation, he would not fail to bring it to light; and in this he fulfilled his promise. The truth is, that arguments and objections, when urged by him, assume a new character, and produce a new effect. He deals not in trite and vague generalities. What had before been thrown out in the gross is thoroughly sifted, and applied to its proper use. Whether intent upon Greek manuscripts, or ancient versions, or early fathers, his power of discrimination is constantly on the alert. Nothing seems to escape him by its minuteness; and yet, whatever subject he is discussing, he places the whole of it before the reader, in all its bearings. Let a man read everything that had been written on the controverted text previously to the time of Mr. Porson, and when he has afterwards perused the 'Letters to Travis,' he will confess *that* to be the

K

work from which he has derived the fullest information on the subject. Such are the effects of great talents, when exercised even on common materials.

"There is one quality of the mind, unnoticed by Bishop Burgess, in which it may be confidently maintained that Mr. Porson 'had no superior' — I mean, the most pure and inflexible love of truth. Under the influence of this principle, he was cautious, and patient, and persevering in his researches; and scrupulously accurate in stating facts as he found them. All who were intimate with him bear witness to this noble part of his character; and his works confirm the testimony of his friends. In a word, if, in a *General Council* of SCHOLARS, an individual were to be selected and sent forth to take a survey of any region of antiquity, profane, or ecclesiastical, it is quite certain that the person who should be found to possess Mr. Porson's endowments would command every vote." *

It would have been pleasant to have taken leave of the Controversy with this very beautiful piece of writing and argument. But transitions are common in this world. From the summits of Parnassus it is not uncommon to be at once precipitated into the bogs and quagmires which surround its base. Crito Cantabrigiensis produced a literary curiosity, — a Reply to a book before it was published; which enabled Crito to notice, in the answered book itself, the answer by anticipation. In acting thus, the author has given the chief proof which he has furnished of his wisdom; for it was certainly much easier to answer Crito before he appeared, than it would have been afterwards. "A Specimen of an intended Publication, which was to have been entitled, a Vindication of them that have the rule over us, for their not

* Pp. 341-348.

having cut out the disputed Passage, 1 John v. 7, 8, from the Authorized Version. Being an Examination of the first six Pages of Professor Porson's IVth Letter to Archdeacon Travis, of the MSS. used by R. Stephens. By Francis Huyshe. London. 1827." 8vo.

The title-page alone of this singular, but vaporing pamphlet, I should think would satisfy most readers of the author's competence for the task he has undertaken. I apprehend, whether Mr. Huyshe is aware of it or not, that the time has passed away when "those who are over us" had an exclusive right to determine what is or is not the Bible. Does the man know that he lives in the nineteenth century? Has he so little acquaintance with "the march of intellect," as to be unaware that the *authority* of the whole bench of bishops is, in such a question, not worth a straw? But to the question, — Mr. Huyshe has paid some attention to it, and, had he possessed a portion of sobriety of mind, might have written what would be worth reading; but he so revels and riots in the subject as to excite serious alarms for the soundness of his intellect. He defends "Stephanus," and his text too, with some ingenuity, though without success, and with little advantage to the apocryphal text. He deals about charges of "falsifying, bandying, and gulling," at a great rate; and "flays and splits open" the false charges preferred by Gibbon and Porson, and so ably answered by Travis and Burgess. What is more, he threatens the world with another visitation. But let his advertisement tell the story of his recent adventures, and of his future exploits, —

> "And when he next doth ride abroad,
> May we be there to see."

"This publication is occasioned by an advertisement in the newspapers, which announced that we might expect a Defence of Mr. Porson against Bishop Burgess, by Crito Cantabrigiensis. My veneration of the abilities and acquirements of Mr. Porson is unbounded: 'forty thousand' sons 'could not, with all their quantity of love, make up my sum.' I can speak of him only, as Dr. Parr does, 'Richard Porson, *του πανυ θαυμαστου*.' But if you talk of 'an invincible love of truth, an inflexible probity,' you sap the foundation of my idolatry; and he stands within the prospect of comparison with his blundering correspondent. The reader has before him a specimen of my reasons for saying, that, if the world was taken captive by him at his will, his own understanding did not bow to that will. And I have to make my grateful acknowledgments to Crito Cantabrigiensis, for his irresistible excitement to this part of my proposed work; as the whole probably would otherwise have been deferred till the night cometh when no man can work. Should he think this not sufficient to establish my opinion, he shall have more of it; and he shall have it too, upon the Complutensian edition, and the Ravian MS.; upon Erasmus's third edition, and the MS. that was sent to him from England; upon the kindred reading discovered in the Montfortian MS.; upon the West African recension; and above all, upon the internal testimony of the passage, — till he cries, 'hold, enough.' But I am not without my hopes that the favor conferred upon me by Crito Cantabrigiensis may be repaid by my saving him the expense of paper and print; and I feel confident of being allowed to doze out whatever may yet remain of the evening of life. without interruption from any other quarter. I have not to learn the truth of what the Trojan lady said,

*λογος γαρ εκ τ' αδοξουντων ιων*
*Κάκ των δοκουντων αυτος ου ταυτον σθενει.*

And I am satisfied with thus publicly entering my protest on these heads; and with having furnished a clew, by which any one who will use a little industry may extricate himself from that labyrinth of fraud, which nearly two centuries have now been constructing round Stephanus and the received text." *

So much importance did the author attach to his performance, — nothing, by the way, peculiar to Mr. Huyshe, — that he transmitted it, with a printed circular, to all "those who have the rule over him." This was like a dutiful son of the Church. We dare say that most of their Lordships would allow him "to doze out the remains of the evening of his life," without interruption on their part, always excepting the ever-watchful Bishop of Salisbury; who certainly would not fail to acknowledge the services of Mr. Huyshe. Crito is, in his usual style, very civil, but very pointed. Whether he has given Mr. Huyshe his quietus, I cannot say, but two years have passed since he last roused himself; from which we should hope that the old gentleman is dozing on his evening very pleasantly. Peace be to his slumbers! May they be lasting and undisturbed!

The following passage, at the end of the Appendix to Crito's Vindication, gives the sum of the Controversy with Mr. Huyshe, and a satisfactory explanation of the whole difficulty on which he makes such a parade of argument.

"We may here, for a moment, revert to the object of all this zeal to have it believed that Robert Stephens had two sets of MSS. — Mr. Huyshe seeing, distinctly enough, that none of the fifteen marked MSS. contained 1 John v. 7, was resolved that Robert Stephens should have MS. authority for the verse; and so, presented him with sixteen additional MSS., some one or more of which contained the verse in the form assigned to it by Stephens's press. Now, let us not attribute to imaginary causes effects which causes known to have existed are sufficient to have produced. The fifth edi-

* Pp. iii., iv.

tion of Erasmus was the basis of Robert Stephens's editions. The Complutensian edition, which was a MS. in Stephens's estimation, contained the disputed passage; and therefore, with him, was authority for its insertion. Erasmus had finally brought the verse into the best shape in which it had then appeared; and accordingly Robert Stephens inserted the verse, with only one variation from the text of Erasmus: — changing τὸ πνεῦμα ἅγιον into τὸ ἅγιον πνεῦμα, which, as a scholar, he knew to be the better Greek, and, as a critic, to be the reading of the Complutensian edition. This surely is an easy and obvious method of accounting for Robert Stephens's proceeding with regard to the verse.

"In subordination to his grand object, Mr. Huyshe has stated his opinions on a variety of topics, the discussion of which would lead me beyond the limits I have prescribed to myself. Whether Stephens's semicircle was misplaced by the collator of the manuscripts, or the compositor of the volume; and whether by accident or from design, — whether the MSS. were collated solely by Henry Stephens, or by Henry Stephens with the assistance of others, — whether Robert Stephens's MS. β was one and the same with the Beza MS. now at Cambridge, or merely 'the same for all critical purposes,' — these points, and others of still less consequence, the reader will easily forgive me if I do not attempt to determine. It may be sufficient to observe that, according to the best of my judgment, the decisions of Mr. Huyshe on these subjects — although accompanied by the most unwarrantable reflections upon the living and the dead — are not often supported by a substantial reason.

"To conclude, Mr. Huyshe has mentioned the Complutensian edition, the third edition of Erasmus, the Berlin and Dublin MSS., the African recension, and the internal evidence, — as matters about which he is quite prepared for ontention. Happily, however, he has given the form of vords by which he may be induced to cherish the thoughts f peace. Availing myself, therefore, of that form, I say, vith the utmost sincerity,—'Hold, Enough.'"*

In defence of himself and of his former publication, the Rev. John Oxlee published, in 1828, "Two Letters, respectully addressed to the Lord Bishop of Salisbury, in defence f certain Positions of the Author, relative to 1 John v. 7; n which, also, the recent Arguments of his Lordship for the Verse are shown to be groundless Surmises, and evident Misakes, as well in Church History as in Criticism." To Mr. Oxlee's views and labors in this Controversy we have aleady adverted. His Lordship had remarked on the temper n which he had conducted the discussion, which was probaly felt to be the more offensive from the weight of Mr. Oxee's talents and learning. In the two letters now addressed o Bishop Burgess, he defends the ground taken in his former Letters very ably and very dispassionately. Every point aderted to by the Bishop, either in his animadversions on Oxee, or otherwise, in support of the passage, is discussed and hown to be either incorrect or inapplicable,—to be founded n ignorance, or to leave out of view some circumstance which ntirely alters its nature,—the new evidence, as well as the ld, is disposed of in a manner that admits not of successful eply. The Montfort MS., the Panoplia Dogmatica of Euhymius Zigabenus, the Complexiones of Cassiodorus, the Critical Edition of Jerome's Version by Vallarsius, the Veona, Harleian, Wolfenbüttel, and other MSS. are shown to fford no satisfactory evidence in support of the passage. The reasoning of his Lordship respecting the Symbolum Antiochenum and Fulgentius is also entirely demolished.

* Crito Cantab., pp. 402-404.

His notice of Mr. Huyshe is worthy of a place in this review.

"Though I cannot congratulate him on the display either of his learning or of his reasoning, nor yet of his modesty, it would be extremely invidious not to notice his prudence and his foresight, in endeavoring to secure to himself the admiration of the bishops; and in furnishing the particulars of his *address*, so that, whenever he shall be wanted, they may know where to find him. The CIRCULAR, he may rest satisfied, for the sake of this one circumstance only, will be carefully deposited amongst the most valuable of their papers. Champions of his calibre, who can dare to penetrate the camp of the enemy, and can fetch away the OPIMA SPOLIA, are invaluable coadjutors in the field of controversy; and, as the Hookers of their day, are sure to be drawn out of their retirement, from their little sequestered parishes, in order to fight the battles of the Church, and to receive at her hands that preferment which she has to bestow, as the reward of their prowess. Indeed, it is scarcely possible to conceive a design more worthy of the pencil than this feat, intimated to us in the circular, of Mr. Huyshe dragging forth to the light completely vanquished and put in chains, that infernal dog PROFESSOR PORSON; whilst, in another part, we behold the OPIMA SPOLIA, modestly laid by our champion at the feet of the Church; who, justly proud of her son, is preparing to decorate his valor with the first honors at her disposal.

"Before taking leave of Mr. Huyshe, I would beg to ask on what Christian principle he has attempted to connect the defence of the disputed passage with that of the Church; and to treat its opponents as inimical to their mother? If I may be allowed to state my own case, I can say with much truth that, in opposing it, I have acted with a view to nothing else than to the honor of the Christian Church. The conduct of

Mr. Huyshe and his fellow-champions is what the fathers of the Church would have universally condemned. They would have deemed it a crime of no ordinary magnitude to deliver to posterity, for the original sacred text, what they themselves had not duly received from their predecessors, nor could find in their Greek manuscripts. Their memory is grossly insulted by the supposition, that they suffered a text of such vast importance in the Trinitarian controversy to be lost from their copies of the Greek Scriptures. The character of the Church docent as the guardian of Holy Writ is no otherwise to be defended, than by denying the possibility of such an occurrence taking place. I maintain, therefore, that in this instance the opponents of the verse are the true sons of the Church; and that they alone deserve well at her hands for having used their best endeavors to remove the interpolation." *

I must now hasten to a conclusion of this lengthened series of articles, by briefly noticing the remaining publications. In the present year appeared, "A Letter to the Rev. Thos. Beynon, Archdeacon of Cardigan, in reply to a Vindication of the Literary Character of Professor Porson, by Crito Cantabrigiensis: and in further proof of the Authenticity of 1 John v. 7. By Thomas Burgess, D.D., Bishop of Salisbury." 8vo. His Lordship's tenacity of life in this cause is certainly the most remarkable feature in his character. He is entitled to much credit for the sincerity and zeal with which he maintains and avows his convictions. But with every disposition to respect his motives and intentions, it is impossible to feel respect for his judgment after so much has been done to produce conviction without any avail. His Lordship persists in repeating the same things, after they have been explained or

* Pp. 120 - 122.

confuted, till his opponents have nothing further to say. In the most unaccountable manner, he converts the negative evidence in opposition to the verse — that is, its absence from manuscripts, versions, and fathers — into positive evidence in its support; and on this strange fallacy builds the principal part of his whole superstructure of defence. There is no arguing with this kind of proof.

The plan of the Bishop's publications is admirably calculated to raise a cloud of dust around the question. It is scarcely possible to get a clear view of it, from the multitude of points which are introduced. For instance, in the last publication, we have first an introduction; then follows a series of tables of contents; then comes a preface of thirty-five pages; after this are forty pages of notes on this introduction; we have then the Letter, which, though announced as the publication, is literally buried between the introduction and the appendix of the work, and is the least part of the whole; after the letter, which consists of thirty-two pages, is a postscript of twenty-two pages; and after TANTUM comes another sort of postscript of thirteen pages more. If this is not writing "about it and about it" till all men may justly be led "to doubt it," we do not know what the tendency of such sort of writing and reasoning is. It is injurious to the Bishop's reputation for learning and candor, and much more injurious to the cause of truth than he seems to be aware of.

Having, I apprehend, tired my readers, and nearly tired myself, I thought here to have shortly summed up and concluded. But I have just procured and read, with all the attention and impartiality in my power, a publication for which Bishop Burgess has expressed many an anxious desire. On which, therefore, I must bestow a few remarks.

"New Criticisms on the celebrated Text, 1 John v. 7. A Synodical Lecture by Francis Anthony Knittel, Counsellor to the Consistory, and General Superintendent of the Grand Duchy of Brunswick Lünebourg. Published at Brunswick in 1785. Translated from the original German, by William Alleyn Evanson, M. A. London." [1829.] 8vo. All parties must feel their obligations to Mr. Evanson for having brought out, in an English translation, this curious work. The subject seems rather a strange one for "a synodical lecture," which I fancy must have been the exemplar of Bishop Burgess, when he made it the subject of a charge to his clergy. That charge, by the by, his Lordship has promised to publish; so that something more may still be expected from the fruitful pen of the Bishop of Salisbury. Had Mr. Evanson not prefixed a preface to Knittel, he would have consulted his reputation as a scholar; had he suppressed the conclusion of it, he would have consulted his reputation as a man of candor and a Christian. That conclusion can sting none but the writer himself. Let him reflect on his own consistency in denouncing the Apocrypha, and yet reading it as the lessons of instruction to the Church of God; protesting against its incorporation and circulation among the inspired Scriptures, and defending a text as certainly spurious as any of the apocryphal books, before he presume to denounce men whose character for integrity and zeal for truth are at least as well known and as much entitled to respect as his own.

Of Knittel, after patiently examining his statements and arguments, I can come to no other conclusion than that at which Michaelis arrived, "that he throws no additional light on the subject." Apart from the controversy, his work contains some useful information on various subjects, elicited with genuine German industry, and set forth with due parade of logic, of learned textual stuffing, and marginal reference and quotation. Under the head of "Greek and Latin Manuscripts discovered which support 1 John v. 7," I expected to find something about MSS. which contained the text; but, to my great surprise, he refers to three MSS. which, by his own account, only swell the number of codices which do not contain the passage. On the first of these manuscripts, after a great many words, he says: —

"This codex augments the list of those which omit 1 John v. 7. At the same time I must observe, that the copyist frequently omits passages of the text of 1 John, but in such a manner as evinces both his negligence and haste; *e. g.* 1 John ii. 22 wants the last words of the verse *τον Πατερα και τον Υἱον*: in like manner, the *πας*, with which verse 23 begins, is wanting. Again, verse 27 wants the conclusion, *μενειτε εν αυτῳ*: verse 28 wants the beginning, *και νυν τεκνια*: 1 John iv. 16 wants the conclusion, *και ὁ Θεος εν αυτῳ*. From these examples, we perceive that the copyist's omission of certain passages of the text may have been occasioned, not always by the various readings of codices, but also by words of similar sound. Therefore *he is not a perfectly safe witness in this matter.*"

On the second he says: —

"This codex may be called *Guelpherbytanus* D. True, its testimony, as far as hitherto known, is of very little weight; but still it contains something remarkable, and deserving further attention."

The reader may accept of these as specimens taken almost at random from this volume, in illustration of the light which is to be found in the "New Criticisms" of the learned Knittel on 1 John v. 7.

Instead of dilating further on this subject myself, I cannot better sum up the whole, than by placing before the reader the following luminous view of the facts which have been elicited and fully established in the course of this extended discussion. The controversy, I should observe, leaves the doctrine of the Trinity unaffected; has tended to establish the authenticity of the inspired writings, and to illustrate the powerful evidence by which their genuineness is ascertained. But till the following positions are fairly met, and satisfactorily answered, it is unnecessary to write or read another book in support of 1 John v. 7.

"There are three ways of ascertaining the genuineness of any particular text of the New Testament; — from its being found in the Greek manuscripts; preserved in the ancient Versions; or cited and commented on in the writings of the fathers. The absence of all this testimony in behalf of the *heavenly witnesses*, your Lordship has been pleased to denominate the *negative* evidence against the verse; whereas I am prepared to maintain, that such testimony is the only *positive* evidence which we can have of any passage either now being, or ever having been, at any time past, a genuine part of the New Testament; and that, in proportion as this sort of evidence either increases or decreases, the genuineness or spuriousness of the passage is rendered more or less doubtful.

"Thus much being premised, it will be no difficult labor to reverse the statement of your Lordship, and to demonstrate to the impartial reader, that since the close of the seventeenth century the novelties of discoveries *against* the passage have been manifold and important; but the novelties *for* it worse than nothing.

"1. Great weight used to be laid on the Greek manuscripts made use of by Robert Stephens for his edition of the Greek Testament; but of that argument we now hear less and less. By the industry of Lelong, Wetstein, Marsh, and Griesbach, most of the manuscripts have been recognized; and afford evidence, not *for*, but *against* the disputed text, in that they contain it not.

"2. During the sixteenth and seventeenth century, the Greek manuscripts consulted, though they all conspired in furnishing evidence against the verse, were but few in number; whereas, by the indefatigable industry of Dr. Griesbach and of other critics of the last century, there are now reckoned up no less than about one hundred and fifty, which have been inspected with a special reference to the passage, and are known not to contain it; whilst, for the verse, there is still extant only the same individual manuscript from which Erasmus, three hundred years ago, so reluctantly interpolated his third edition of the Greek Scriptures. The Codex Ravianus cannot be considered as an exception; being evidently posterior to the invention of printing, and even copied from the Complutensian Polyglot.

"3. By the labor of Mr. Porson and other critics, the fact has been ascertained, that in no Greek manuscript, hitherto examined, are the words ἐν τῇ γῇ found making a part of the eighth, and indicating the loss of the seventh verse; so that one chief argument formerly made use of has been wholly done away with.

"4. The Syriac Version, which in antiquity and authority may well contend with the Latin, though it made its appearance without the foisted text, had been printed in a manner from one or two manuscripts only; so that there might still have remained a rational doubt, whether at some future time the passage would not be found in some of the Syriac as well as of the Latin manuscripts. But, within the last century, a multitude of Syriac manuscripts, in various parts of Christendom, have been examined, and still found not to contain it; so that the evidence arising from this most ancient version has become much more decisive than it was.

"5. In the beginning of the eighteenth century there came forth, edited on the authority of various manuscripts, the Coptic Version of the New Testament. This version, in the opinion of the learned editor himself, was made from the Greek in the beginning of the third century; and since it coincides, as well in the Sahidic as in the Memphitic dialect, with the existing state of the Greek manuscripts, it has contributed much to the evidence against the disputed text, and that, too, within the last century; Mill being about the first of our sacred critics who had the opportunity to mention it.

"6. Of the erroneous persuasion respecting its existence in the Armenian Version, even till after the time of Mill, I have already taken notice. Neither Porson, nor Griesbach, nor Marsh professes to have understood anything of the Armenian tongue themselves; but they correctly judged that the passage had been foisted into it contrary to the authority of its manuscripts. In my Letters to Mr. Nolan I have afforded, what your Lordship will not easily find elsewhere, some more certain information respecting the state of the Armenian text; and have there demonstrated its evidence to be not *for*, but wholly *against* the authority of the verse; and that its appearance in the printed edition of Uscan was an interpolation from the Latin.

"7. The Philoxenian, or later Syriac, is another independent version; and wholly distinct from the *Simplex*. It was made at the first, probably, from manuscripts of the fifth century; and afterwards collated with others a century or two later. Since the translation is highly literal, it has preserved to us, with the utmost certainty, the state of the Greek text at the time of its being made. It retains, however, no trace of the *heavenly witnesses;* and, as the whole of this version of the New Testament was not published till within these thirty years, it may well be considered as novel evidence against the verse, and that in the course of the last century.

"8. I profess to have no acquaintance with the Slavonic Version myself; but to the learned its history is not unknown: that it was made from the Greek towards the close of the ninth century; and afterwards either amended or retranslated, in the thirteenth or fourteenth, by Alexius, the Metropolitan. In this version from the Greek, as well as in all others which have the least pretensions to antiquity, the text of the *heavenly witnesses* is said to be absent; and, since all the critical inquiries into the state of the Slavonic are of a very recent date, its evidence against the passage must be regarded as another novelty within the period prescribed.

"9. Before the commencement of the preceding century, the Prologue to the Catholic Epistles was universally believed to have had Jerome for its author. Neither Socinus nor any of his immediate followers ever dared to question its authenticity; and, though they objected to the text of the *heavenly witnesses*, they were constrained to acknowledge that at least Jerome, the ablest critic of the fourth century, had publicly defended it. But since the works of Jerome have been more accurately and critically edited, that document has been judged to be the forgery of some sophisticator of the sixth or seventh century; and there is scarcely a critic to be found, since the time of Mill, who has not added his voice to that sentence of condemnation. Behold, then, within the last hundred years, another novelty against the verse; and that of great weight and importance.

"10. It is equally well known to the learned, that, before the close of the seventeenth century, the books to Theophilus, in which the passage under dispute once or twice appears, were usually ascribed to Athanasius, whose title they bear before them. But since the publication of the Benedictine edition of his works, in which these spurious tracts are more pointedly condemned, and separated from the genuine, the authority of Athanasius for the verse has ceased to be brought forward.

"11. In all the more ancient Latin tracts containing any trace of it, including the books to Theophilus on the Trinity, and the *Liber adversus Varimadum*, there are circumstances attending its insertion which clearly indicate that the writers themselves were wholly ignorant of its existence as a text of Scripture; whilst, as I have shown in my Letters to Mr. Nolan, they furnish the very best evidence against its authenticity, in that the words are adduced, not as the very language, but only as the *demonstrated sense* of the language of St. John.

"12. The supposed citation of it by Fulgentius is an argument on which, up to this very hour, great stress has been laid. But, in my Letters to Mr. Nolan, I have alleged some strong reasons to prove, that for its appearance in the *Responsio contra Arrianos* we are probably indebted, not to any knowledge which the learned father himself had of the text, but to the dexterity of Cochlæus. I have been informed of a late edition of the works of Fulgentius, printed at Venice, in 1742; the editor of which professes to have collated manuscripts, &c., but I have not been able to procure a copy of it. To that editor, then, the reader must be referred for more satisfactory information on the point at issue; and, if he finds nothing more in its behalf than the authority of the *editio princeps* of Cochlæus, the supposed testimony of Fulgentius must take its place beside that of Jerome, as being equally bottomed in fraud and mistake.

"Such, my Lord, are the novelties or discoveries against the verse in the course of the last century. They are of such a nature as to leave its advocates not so much as one firm prop on which to rest their defence; and have fairly reduced them to the dire necessity of fetching from the works of the fathers a few *coincidences* of thought and expression, which they would be happy to palm on our credulity for *allusions* to the text. To one already conversant in the history of this dispute, a minute detail of what has been going on may seem tedious and void of interest; but the extraordinary statement of your Lordship, that the cumulative evidence of modern date had brought nothing important against the verse, in addition to the materials of Sandius and Simon, was not otherwise to be refuted than by an appeal to these facts." *

After the preceding sheets had been printed, and published in the work in which they originally appeared, I received another pamphlet on the controversy, which bears strong evidence of proceeding from the pen of Crito Cantabrigiensis, though it appears under another designation: "Remarks upon Mr. Evanson's Preface to his Translation of Knittel's New Criticisms on 1 John v. 7. By Clemens Anglicanus. Cambridge, 1829."

The author of this acute and well-written tract does not enter into the general discussion with Knittel. This he deemed unnecessary, as every argument adduced by the learned German deserving of attention had been disposed of before. His attention is exclusively directed to the preface, the misstatements and inaccuracies of which he has detected and exhibited in a manner that, I should suppose, will make the translator regret he ever attempted anything original on a subject he so imperfectly understands. Clemens Anglicanus, at the same time, writes in the most gentlemanly manner. With the most perfect command of his temper and his pen, he analyses Mr. Evanson's reasonings, and entirely demolishes them. Without quoting a large part of the pamphlet, I could not place the argument of it before the reader,

* Oxlee's Two Letters to the Bishop of Salisbury, pp. 13 – 18.

so as to enable him to appreciate its merits. I must, therefore, content myself with extracting the concluding paragraphs, in which he gives his opinion of Knittel's work, and of part of his translator's preface. Those who wish to examine the subject more fully, will refer to the pamphlet itself; or to a very able critique on Knittel and Clemens Anglicanus in the Eclectic Review for the present month, (February, 1830).

"Mr. Evanson has done good service by his translation of the 'New Criticisms.' M. Knittel, the author of the work, is manifestly a very learned man; but his ingenuity — perhaps I might say, his imagination — fairly overpowers his judgment. He finds scarcely anything but resemblances between objects which present to the common eye little besides dissimilitude. The consequence is, that his book contains as weak arguments, perhaps, as ever were advanced in favor of the disputed text; but they are frequently managed with uncommon dexterity. He affects, in his discussion, the smartness of dialogue, and is somewhat rhapsodical in his style of writing. The best part of his book relates to Cyprian. As for his argument depending upon the *ἓν τὰ τρία* and *τὰ τρία ἕν*, — which, from Griesbach's notice, we were previously aware that Knittel had employed, — it only shows that the Greek fathers who used such expressions were accustomed to express, in the briefest manner, the received doctrine of a Trinity in Unity. . . . . Let me add, that I think it much to be lamented that the translator should have retained the algebraical proof or illustration of the doctrine just mentioned, — which forms appendix (G). . . . . That the 'New Criticisms' present no very distinct view of the subject discussed, may, I think, be collected from Mr. Evanson's preface. Had Mr. Evanson translated any one of the dissertations of Mill, Bengelius, Wetstein, or Griesbach, his preface could scarcely have contained so many inaccuracies.

"Mr. Evanson devotes several pages of his preface to observations on the mode of criticism adopted by 'the Deistical Wetstein, the Pelagian, Utilitarian Semler, and their servile imitators'; from the tenor of which observations I naturally conclude that he does not aspire after the character of a discreet and temperate writer.

"Mr. Evanson apprehends that 'the transition, from *our* conclusion to that of the Unitarians is natural and easy.'—'*You*,' says the learned writer, 'reject one verse of John's First Epistle: *they* reject the first fourteen verses of his Gospel.'—'It is,' he adds, 'but a step, and we reject the Sacred Canon altogether.' Now the only method, as it appears to me, by which all this can be effected, must be by disregarding our present Greek manuscripts, as '*few* and *suspicious* witnesses'; and referring to 'the many thousand uncollated Greek manuscripts which are probably in existence.' If the Unitarians should manifest any disposition to take this course, which has been chosen by Mr. Evanson himself, I trust that he will be able to produce good reasons why they ought not to follow his example."*

I should have stated, in the regular course of the memoirs, the views taken of the controverted passage by Mr. Horne, in his valuable Introduction to the Scriptures,—a work no less distinguished for the laborious diligence which it displays, than for the amiable candor which pervades it. Of this the present controversy affords an illustration. In his earlier editions, the mind of the author either hung in doubt, or it leaned to the side of the authenticity of the passage. In his sixth edition, however, he fairly surrenders it, as no longer defensible. After giving, which he had done in all his editions, an admirable statement of the evidence on both sides, he concludes thus:—

* Clemens Anglicanus's Remarks, pp. 44-46.

"Upon a review of all the preceding arguments, the disputed clause (we think) must be abandoned as spurious: nor can anything less than the positive authority of *unsuspected* manuscripts justify the admission of so important a passage into the sacred canon. Much stress, it is true, has been laid upon some points in the internal evidence, and particularly the supposed grammatical arguments (Nos. 2 and 3), and the reasons assigned for the omission of this clause. But some of these reasons have been shown to be destitute of the support alleged in their behalf; and the remainder are wholly hypothetical, and unsustained by any satisfactory evidence. Internal evidence,' indeed, (as Bishop Marsh forcibly argues,) 'may show that a passage is *spurious*, though external evidence is in its favor; for instance, if it contain allusions to things which did not exist in the time of the reputed author. BUT NO INTERNAL EVIDENCE CAN PROVE A PASSAGE TO BE GENUINE, WHEN EXTERNAL EVIDENCE IS DECIDEDLY AGAINST IT. A spurious passage may be fitted to the context as well as a genuine passage. No arguments, therefore, from internal evidence, however ingenious they may appear, can outweigh the mass of external evidence which applies to the case in question.'" *

I must not omit to mention, that Mr. Horne was the first, so far as I have observed, to bring before the British public the testimony of the *Codex Ottobonianus*, as containing the disputed clause. It adds, however, nothing to the authority of the passage. The following is his account of this manuscript, derived from Professor Scholz's communication in the "Biblisch-Kritische Reise."

"The *Codex Ottobonianus* 298, in the Vatican Library, is the only other manuscript in which the disputed clause is to be found. According to Dr. Scholz it is as follows: οτι τρεις

* Horne's Introduction, Vol. IV. p. 485.

*εισιν οι μαρτυρουντες απο του ουρανου, πατηρ, λογος, και πνευμα αγιον· και οι τρεις εις το εν εισι. Και τρεις εισιν οι μαρτυρουντες απο της γης, το πνευμα,* &c., &c. It is worthy of remark that this manuscript has *απο του ουρανου, from heaven,* instead of *εν τῳ ουρανῳ, in heaven,* and *απο της γης, from earth,** instead of *εν τῃ γῃ, on earth,* which words occur in the Codex Montfortianus; and the absence of the article (as in that manuscript) before the words expressive of Father, Son, and Holy Ghost, manifestly indicates the Latin origin of the *Codex Ottobonianus;* which has further been altered in many places to make it agree with the Latin Vulgate. And as this manuscript is stated to have been written in the fifteenth century, this late date, in addition to the very doubtful internal evidence which it affords, renders its testimony of no force whatever." †

* [Horne has been led into error by Scholz. The manuscript reads ἐπὶ τῆς γῆς, *on earth,* instead of ἀπὸ τῆς γῆς, as appears by the fac-simile given in the later editions of Horne's Introduction. — ED.]

† Horne's Introduction, Vol IV. p. 465.

# APPENDIX

## BY THE EDITOR.

THE principal object of the following Appendix is to continue the history of the controversy respecting 1 John v. 7, from the year 1830, the date of Mr. Orme's Memoir, to the present time. Notice will also be taken of some earlier publications on the subject.

THE Monthly Anthology and Boston Review for February, 1811, contained an article on Griesbach's Greek Testament, now known to have been written by the Rev. Joseph S. Buckminster, in which the question was asked, "To what is it to be attributed that even at the present day 1 John v. 7 is quoted in proof of the doctrine of the Trinity, and even taken as a text of discourses, when it ought to be known that it has not more authority in its favor than the famous reading of the seventh commandment, in one of the editions of King James's Bible: *Thou shalt commit adultery?*" (p. 110.) This strong statement, followed by a remark placing Acts xx. 28 and 1 Tim. iii. 16 in the same category, gave occasion to a critical discussion of the various readings of these passages in the Panoplist for April and May, 1811, the latter of the two articles being mainly devoted to 1 John v. 7. The writer in the Panoplist, while admitting "great doubts" respecting this passage, urges the quotation of the text in the Confession of Faith presented by the Catholic bishops to Huneric, A. D. 484, and the use of the article before ἓν in the last clause of the eighth verse, as important arguments for its genuineness; and observes: "Until these [circumstances] are fairly considered and fairly explained, we cannot deem the spuriousness of the passage to be settled beyond dispute." (p. 539.) The argument on the former point is quoted from Charles Butler's Letters to Professor Marsh, and on the latter from Middleton's work on the Greek Article. In the Anthology for June, 1811, Mr. Buckminster replied, remarking that there was "not a single argument in Mr. Butler's letter, which had not been already brought forward by Travis, and considered by Porson and Griesbach"; and propounding four questions, which he says the advocates of the verse must answer, before this African Confession can be offered as good authority for the existence of the verse in Latin copies at the end of the fifth century. The argument that the use of the article before ἕν implies the existence of a previous ἕν, to be found only in ver. 7, he meets by referring to the use of τὸ ἕν in Phil. ii. 2. The Panoplist for August, 1811, contains a rejoinder; but there is no reply to the four questions, nor any notice of the passage adduced in illustration of the use of the article before ἕν.

In the year 1820 the Rev. Henry Ware, Jr., published "Two Letters to the Rev. Alexander McLeod, D. D., Pastor of the Reformed Presbyterian Church, containing Remarks upon the Texts from which he preached on the Evenings of April 30, and May 7." New York, 1820, 8vo. pp. 24. The text of Dr. McLeod's first discourse was 1 John v. 7, which was assumed to be genuine. Mr. Ware protests against this assumption, and quotes in opposition the concessions of a number of eminent Trinitarian writers, who had expressed in the strongest terms their conviction of its spuriousness. Among these quotations, the following extract from a Latin letter of Bishop Lowth to Michaelis, first published in Michaelis's *Literarischer Briefwechsel*, or "Literary Correspondence," Vol. II. p. 428, may deserve to be repeated here, as the work from which it was taken is probably accessible to few English readers. "We have," says the Bishop, "some wranglers in theology, sworn to follow their master, who are prepared to defend anything, however absurd, should there be occasion. But I believe there is no one among us in the least degree conversant with sacred criticism, and having the use of his understanding, who would be willing to contend for the genuineness of the verse, 1 John v. 7."* In 1823 a third edition of Mr. Ware's tract was

* "Habemus in theologia rabulas quosdam in magistri alicujus verba juratos; nihil est tam absurdum quod illi, si res et occasio ferat, non

published in Boston, with additions; and it is reprinted in his Works, Vol. II. pp. 303-330, Boston, 1846, 12mo.

The British Critic, Quarterly Theological Review and Ecclesiastical Record for July, 1828, Vol. IV. pp. 1-32, in a review of the Vindication of Porson by *Crito Cantabrigiensis*, contains a full and able discussion of the genuineness of the disputed text. Speaking of Bishop Burgess, the reviewer says: — "In the various publications enumerated above, he has brought forward, indeed, almost every argument, good, bad, and indifferent, that has ever suggested itself to any of the defenders of the verse, and has most entirely failed of producing the desired effect. The causes of this bad success are not to be looked for in the want of zeal and talents in the advocate, but in the utter hopelessness of the cause which he has attempted to maintain." (pp. 2, 3.) The British Critic was at this time the leading organ of the High Church party in England.

In 1828 Karl Rickli published a commentary, in German, on the First Epistle of John, with the following title: — "The First Epistle of John, explained and applied in Sermons delivered before the Evangelical Reformed Church at Lucerne, with an Historical Preface, and an Exegetical Appendix." * He rejects 1 John v. 7 without hesitation as spurious, and gives in his Appendix (pp. 29-44) an interesting account of its introduction into the various modern translations of the New Testament. He states that the verse was regarded as supposititious by Luther, Zwingli, Œcolampadius, Bullinger, and Bugenhagen; that it did not appear in Luther's version till 1593, (not 1574 as erroneously stated by Panzer and others,) when it was inserted in the edition printed at Frankfort, from which the corruption rapidly spread, and after 1620 became universal. This interpolation of Luther's

parati sint defendere. Sed neminem credo jam apud nos esse, in critica sacra paulum modo versatum, et cui sanum sit sinciput, qui pro sinceritate commatis 7mi 1 Joh: v. propugnare velit." — See Christian Disciple for March, 1819; New Series, I. 109.

* "Johannis erster Brief, erklärt und angewendet in Predigten, . . . mit historischem Vorbericht, und exegetischem Anhange." . . . . Luzern, 1828, 8vo. pp. xxxiv., 399, 48.

version was in direct opposition to his solemn charge, in the Preface to the edition published in the year of his death (1546), that no alteration should be made in his work. The first edition of his translation of the New Testament was published in 1522.

In 1831 another volume appeared from the pen of the indefatigable Bishop Burgess, entitled "Remarks on the General Tenour of the New Testament regarding the Nature and Dignity of Jesus Christ, addressed to Mrs. Joanna Baillie," in which, of course, the genuineness of 1 John v. 7 was defended; and in 1835 he published at Salisbury the following work: "An Introduction to the Controversy on the Disputed Verse of St. John, as revived by Mr. Gibbon: to which is added Christian Theocracy: a Second Letter to Mrs. Joanna Baillie." The Introduction was first privately printed in 1833. It throws no new light on the subject.

In 1835 Cardinal Wiseman published at Rome "Two Letters on some Parts of the Controversy concerning the Genuineness of 1 John v. 7: containing also an Inquiry into the Origin of the first Latin Version of Scripture, commonly called 'the Itala.'" These Letters first appeared in the Catholic Magazine for 1832 and 1833, Vols. II. and III. The Roman edition contains some additions. They are reprinted, with a few verbal changes, in Vol. I. of Wiseman's Essays on Various Subjects, London, 1853; and this is the edition from which I shall quote.

In these Letters the Cardinal maintains that the first Latin version of the Greek Testament originated in the Roman province of North Africa; that the so-called *interpretatio Itala*, which Augustine preferred for its closeness and perspicuity, was a revision or recension of this primary Latin version, and consequently inferior in critical authority. He further maintains that, though the disputed passage was wanting in the manuscripts used in Italy, and does not appear in the writings of the Italian fathers, it belonged to the original Latin version, made in Africa; whence "we are led to conclude that the manuscripts used in making this version possessed the verse; and these were necessarily manuscripts of far greater antiquity than any we can now inspect." *

* Wiseman's Essays, I. 66.

That the passage in question belonged originally to the Old Latin version, Dr. Wiseman infers from its being quoted or referred to by the African fathers, Tertullian, Cyprian, Marcus Celedensis, Victor Vitensis, the four hundred bishops assembled under Huneric at Carthage, Vigilius Tapsensis, and Fulgentius. A new argument in favor of this thesis is based on an anonymous work called the *Speculum*, or "Mirror," found in a manuscript assigned by Wiseman to the sixth or seventh century, belonging to the library of Santa Croce in Gerusalemme in Rome. This work consists wholly of quotations from Scripture, arranged under one hundred and forty-four heads, embracing the chief points of Christian belief and practice. The text is that of the Old Latin version, and generally agrees with the quotations of the African fathers. It has been published by Cardinal Mai in his Nova Bibliotheca Patrum, Tom. I. Pars II., Rome, 1852, 4to. No title is given to the manuscript by the original transcriber, but several different and later hands have prefixed inscriptions erroneously identifying it with a treatise of Augustine's against the Donatists, which Possidius, in his list of that father's works, entitles *De Testimoniis Scripturarum contra Donatistas et Idola*. One of the four titles, however, thus prefixed to the work, reads simply *Libri de Speculo*. We know that Augustine made a collection of practical extracts from Scripture which bore the name of *Speculum*, serving the reader as a "mirror" of character; and Wiseman and Mai argue that the present compilation is no other than that work. To discuss the question fully, and to consider the comparative claims of the two other *Specula* which have been attributed by different editors to Augustine, would occupy too much space. I would only observe that compilations of this kind were peculiarly liable to alteration and interpolation by transcribers,* and that there are strong presumptions against the supposi-

* For an illustration of this fact we need go no further than the work which forms a part of the same manuscript which contains the *Speculum*, namely, Cyprian's *Testimonia adversus Judæos*. The Benedictine editors complain that the manuscripts of this work vary so much, that it is impossible to determine what part of it is Cyprian's. — Cypriani Opera, Paris, 1726, fol., p. 596.

tion that Augustine was the author of the present work in its present form. The *Speculum* of Augustine, as his biographer Possidius informs us, was accompanied by a Preface; this has none: Augustine in his quotations from the Old Latin version used the Italian text; in this the African recension is followed: Augustine has not only never quoted 1 John v. 7 in his voluminous writings, but his comments on the verse following show that he cannot have been acquainted with it; in this *Speculum* it is quoted twice.*

Dr. Tregelles well remarks, that "even if all Wiseman's primary positions were good, they would only show that some *Latin* copies had the passage very early. An addition in some one version is of itself *no* authority for the adoption of the passage as genuine."† But the reasoning of Dr. Wiseman rests on assumptions altogether false. The pretended unanimity of the African fathers in support of the verse is purely imaginary. The supposed allusion to 1 John v. 7 in Tertullian, the earliest Latin father, really "furnishes," as Bishop Kaye has observed, "most decisive proof that he knew nothing of the verse";‡ the supposed quotation from Cyprian proves nothing to the purpose, and other portions of his writings raise a very strong presumption against his acquaintance with the disputed text;§ the passage adduced from Marcus Celedensis contains no quotation, and affords no ground for the supposition that he knew the text of the Three Heavenly Witnesses; a later African father, Facundus, was clearly ignorant of it, and derives the doctrine of the Trinity from a mystical interpretation of the eighth verse, as Augustine had done before him. The earliest quotation of the text is to be

* Once in connection with the eighth verse, which precedes the seventh, as follows: — "Quoniam tres sunt qui testimonium dicunt in terra, spiritus, aqua, et sanguis; et hii tres unum sunt in Christo Jesu. Et tres sunt qui testimonium dicunt in caelo, Pater, Verbum, et Spiritus; et hii tres unum sunt." (Cap. 2; see also c. 3.)

† Textual Criticism of the New Testament, in Horne's Introduction, 10th edition, IV. 363, 364.

‡ Ecclesiastical History, etc., illustrated from the Writings of Tertullian, 3d edition, p. 515.

§ On this point see *Crito Cantabrigiensis*, Vindication of Porson, pp. 381–385.

found in the writings of Vigilius Tapsensis, in the latter part of the fifth century; and from that time it appears with such a variety of readings as to suggest at once its character as an interpolation, derived from a marginal gloss. Its occurrence in the *Speculum* proves only that it existed in some Latin manuscripts as early as the seventh century.

Dr. Wiseman further gives an account of a manuscript of the Latin Vulgate preserved in the Benedictine monastery of La Cava, which contains the text of the Three Heavenly Witnesses, but with some peculiar readings. Cardinal Mai regards it as belonging to the seventh century at latest; Tischendorf assigns it to the eighth.

The Cardinal finally entertains us with some *reports* of *Greek* manuscripts containing the passage. He states that in the Angelica Library at Rome is preserved the copy of the Bible used by Angelo Rocca, the secretary of the Congregation appointed by Clement VII. for the correction of the Vulgate. Upon the text of St. John in this volume is the following marginal note:—"Hæc verba sunt certissime de textu et allegantur contra hæreticos ab Athanasio, Gregorio Nazianzeno, Cyrillo et Cypriano; et Hieronymus in prologo dicit ab infidelibus scriptoribus fuisse prætermissa. In Græco etiam quodam antiquissimo exemplari quod habetur Venetiis leguntur; unde colligitur Græca, quæ passim feruntur, in hac parte esse mendosa, et omnia Latina manuscripta in quibus non habentur illa verba signata." * That is, "These words certainly belong to the text, and are alleged against the heretics by Athanasius, Gregory Nazianzen, Cyril, and Cyprian; and Jerome in his Prologue says they were omitted by unfaithful transcribers. They are also read in a very ancient Greek copy preserved at Venice; whence it is inferred that the ordinary Greek copies are faulty in this place, and likewise all the Latin manuscripts in which the marked words are not contained."

On this statement it may be sufficient to quote the remarks of Dr. William Wright, in the Appendix to his translation of Seiler's Biblical Hermeneutics, pp. 635, 636:—"But we know that it

* Wiseman's Essays, I. 68.

was *not* quoted by Athanasius, nor by Gregory Nazianzen, nor by Cyril; and that Jerome did not write the Prologue, which was forged three or four hundred years after that father was dead. The Greek copy at Venice has also long since shrunk from inspection."

In regard to this Greek copy at Venice I would venture the conjecture that it is the manuscript belonging to the Library of St. Mark, described by Bishop Burnet in his Travels in a passage already quoted in this volume (pp. 14, 15). This manuscript contains the Acts and Epistles in Greek, Latin, and Arabic. It is numbered 96 in Scholz's list of manuscripts of the Acts and Catholic Epistles, and is assigned by him to the eleventh century. The text of the Three Heavenly Witnesses is found in it, but unfortunately *only in the Latin portion*, which is taken from the Vulgate.*

Dr. Wiseman next adduces the oral testimony of a gentleman, Don Leopoldo Sebastiani, who had travelled over a great part of Greece expressly with the view of collating manuscripts of the New Testament for a Latin version of it, which he afterwards published. "His statement is, that he has seen several manuscripts with the verse erased, and two in which it is written *prima manu*, in the margin. One was at Nicosia in Cyprus, in possession of a Greek of abilities, a merchant as I understood him. It was in uncial letters, large; on the margin, by the same hand, although in smaller characters, was the verse, with an annotation that it belonged to the text."†

The hope expressed by Dr. Wiseman that "some traveller may be able to verify this testimony" has not yet been realized.

These Letters of Cardinal Wiseman are a valuable contribution to the history of the Old Latin version; but scholars generally, I think, will acquiesce in the judgment of the North British Review, that, in respect to 1 John v. 7, "his vindication is merely a piece of feeble ingenuity, — designed at the same time to uphold the authority of the Latin or Romish Church."‡ It is worthy of

* See Rinck's Lucubratio Critica, pp. 30, 41, 109.

† Wiseman's Essays, I. 68, 69.

‡ North British Review, Aug. 1853; XIX. 435.

note that the prudent Cardinal, though presenting certain arguments in favor of the disputed text, "as materials for scholars to consider," nowhere expresses a positive belief in its genuineness. He professes to treat only of "some parts of the controversy."

It should be here mentioned, perhaps, that Cardinal Angelo Mai, in his note on the passage of the *Speculum* before referred to, contends for the genuineness of 1 John v. 7, — it being sanctioned, in his view, by "a solemn decree" of the Council of Trent, — and says, pathetically, "I am deeply grieved that some celebrated editors of the present age have not hesitated to omit this verse, and have thus thrown away an excellent weapon against the Socinians and Antichristians." * There is no argument in the note that calls for remark, except perhaps the extraordinary blunder of referring to Wetstein's Greek Testament as an authority in favor of the genuineness of the passage. Cardinal Mai has rendered great service to literature by the publication of manuscripts which might otherwise have long remained entombed in the Vatican; his industry was indefatigable; but he has a poor reputation among scholars for critical acumen and accuracy.

In 1833 - 35 the Rev. Francis Huyshe, who has been already introduced to us by Mr. Orme, published a long series of articles in the British Magazine, Vols. III. - VII., entitled "A Vindication of the Early Parisian Greek Press," which have a bearing on the evidence for 1 John v. 7, the writer maintaining that the passage must have been contained in one or more of the manuscripts used by Robert Stephens (Estienne) for his editions of the Greek Testament printed in 1546, 1549, and 1550. Mr. Huyshe also published in the same magazine, Vol. V. pp. 702 - 707, a notice of Dr. Wiseman's Letters on 1 John v. 7. His baseless hypotheses were demolished by the Rev. John Oxlee in three articles printed in the British Magazine, 1835, Vol. VII. pp. 60 - 63, 298 - 302, and 544 - 549.

The Rev. William Wright, LL. D., of Trinity College, Dublin, published in 1835 a translation of Seiler's Biblical Hermeneutics, with additional notes. He treats of the disputed passage in an Appendix to the volume, pp. 613 - 652, which is valuable for its

* Mai's Nova Bibl. Patrum, Tom. I. Pars II. p. 7.

full account of the readings of the Latin manuscripts, and its refutation of some of Wiseman's arguments. In regard to the *Speculum* he observes: —

"Dr. Wiseman is further of opinion, that, under any circumstances, whoever might have been the author of this anonymous work, the use of the old version will not allow us to assign it to a much later age than the middle of the fourth century.

"But Pope Leo the Great made use of the old version in the fifth century, and even of an impure copy; and Gregory the Great, in the sixth century, says that he used at one time the old, at another the new version, just as the one or the other happened to be better adapted to demonstration, since the apostolical chair, which he filled, recognized both. — *Letter to Leander, Bishop of Seville.*" *

In the Literary and Theological Review (New York) for March, 1835, Vol. II. pp. 141 – 148, there is an article on the "Authenticity of 1 John v. 7, 8," by the Rev. William W. Hunt, of Amherst, Mass., in which the genuineness of the passage is maintained. The essay is not creditable to the learning or ability of the author. His acquaintance with the subject may be judged of by the assertions that the words ἐν τῇ γῇ in the eighth verse are "generally allowed to be genuine," and "found in some early Greek manuscripts"; and that "there is not a little evidence that the passage is quoted or referred to by distinguished Greek writers of the third or fourth century, and it is found in *all the printed editions of the Greek Testament!*" (pp. 143, 145, 146.) The following is mentioned among the considerations which should incline us to receive the disputed text: — "The Bible is the revelation of God, and the only one which he has given to men. . . . It is immensely important that this book, as a whole, have all the weight of Divine authority. Now what is the influence upon the community of rejecting a part of it, — of calling a verse, here and there, spurious? Other verses are soon suspected, especially if they reveal an unpleasant doctrine, or inculcate an unpleasant duty. The public confidence is shaken, and infidelity is encouraged." (p. 147.)

In 1836 Dr. J. M. A. Scholz, Professor of Theology in the

* Seiler's Biblical Hermeneutics, p. 634.

University of Bonn, published at Leipsic the second volume of his edition of the Greek Testament, for which he had examined, more or less, several hundreds of manuscripts which had never before been used for critical purposes. Though a Catholic, and though, as Archbishop Kenrick remarks in the note on 1 John v. 7 in his translation of the New Testament, the genuineness of this verse is generally maintained by Catholics, "being read in the Vulgate, which, in all its parts, was sanctioned by the Council of Trent," Scholz rejects the disputed passage as spurious, as he had before done in his German translation of the New Testament, published in 1830. This gave occasion to "Three Letters to the Rev. Dr. Scholz . . . on the Contents of his Note on 1 John v. 7. By the Bishop of Salisbury." Southampton, 1837, 8vo. In these Letters, which were privately printed, Bishop Burgess, as we are told by his biographer, "pointed out some remarkable contradictions between certain passages in the Prolegomena to that work [Scholz's edition of the Greek Testament] and the statements of his note on 1 John v. 7, respecting the age and date of the Greek MSS. containing the disputed verse." We are further informed that Dr. Scholz "acknowledged, in very respectful terms, the receipt of the letters; he observed that the MS. [MSS.] in question [the *Codex Ottobonianus* 298, and a Neapolitan manuscript which has the verse in the margin in a handwriting of the sixteenth or seventeenth century] added something to the evidence in favor of the authenticity of the verse, but maintained that they were of very little weight when compared in authority and antiquity with the multitude omitting it." *

In 1845 the Rev. Frederick A. Farley published a tract entitled "Grounds for rejecting the Text of the Three Heavenly Witnesses; I. John, v. 7. With Concessions of Trinitarians upon the Same." Boston, April, 1845, 12mo. pp. 24. This was printed for the American Unitarian Association as No. 213 of the First Series of its "Tracts." The author acknowledges his great indebtedness for his materials to Mr. John Wilson's "Concessions of Trinitarians," Manchester, Eng., 1842, 8vo; a remarkable work, to which I would also refer the curious reader for some

* Harford's Life of Bishop Burgess, p. 477.

Trinitarian authorities for rejecting the disputed passage, which it does not seem worth while to mention here.

In 1858 Dr. Joseph Turnbull published in London "The Seven Epistles of James, Peter, John, and Jude, and the Revelation. Translated from the Original Greek, with Critical Notes, and a Dissertation on 1 John v. 7, 8." This dissertation, which maintains the genuineness of the passage, was reviewed by Dr. S. P. Tregelles in the Journal of Sacred Literature and Biblical Record for April, 1858, pp. 167-178. He remarks:— "Dr. Turnbull's dissertation has one merit,—brevity,—for it is rather less than *ten* pages; but in these ten pages there is hardly a statement that is worthy of implicit confidence. This may sound like a harsh judgment, but I will give proofs." (p. 168.) The proofs given are ample. There is nothing new in Dr. Turnbull's dissertation but mistakes, one of the most remarkable of which is an argument for the genuineness of the passage founded on its supposed existence in a Wolfenbüttel manuscript assigned by Griesbach to the eleventh or twelfth century. Dr. Turnbull has confounded the *Codex Guelpherbytanus* XVI. 7, (No. 69 in the Acts and Catholic Epistles,) to which Griesbach assigns the date above mentioned, and which *omits* the disputed text, (though it has been added in the margin by a very recent hand,) with the *Codex Guelpherbytanus* D, described by Knittel, which contains it, but also contains in the same handwriting the Latin versions of Vatable, Castalio, and Beza, showing that it was not written before the latter part of the sixteenth century.* This blunder is accompanied with censure of Griesbach for supposed inconsistency in his account of the manuscript; on which Tregelles quaintly remarks:—

"Griesbach was certainly right in each thing that he said; but if an extract from a catalogue at the beginning of a volume may be made the nominative case to a verb at the end of the book, then will no author be safe."

In respect to another point Tregelles observes:—"Dr. Turnbull next seeks, by mere assertion and by a reference to an in-

* See Griesbach's *Diatribe* on 1 John v. 7, p. 7; Knittel's *Neue Kritiken*, or "New Criticisms," pp. 124, 127.

correct statement of Dr. Adam Clarke, to claim a high place for the Codex Montfortianus at Dublin. I have recently discussed this manuscript (see Horne's Introd. IV. 213 – 217), and therefore I shall now only repeat that it contains the Latin chapters; that in other parts of the chapter 1 John v. it shows that its accordance with Latin copies is peculiar; that the Gospels could not be older than the latter part of the *fifteenth* century; the Epistles and Acts were afterwards added (sometime between the year 1500 and the middle of the reign of Elizabeth); and that last of all the Apocalypse was appended in the reign of that queen." *

The Boston Review for May, 1864, Vol. IV. pp. 258 – 273, contains an article on "The Greek Text in Acts, xx. 28; 1 Timothy, iii. 16; and 1 John, v. 7, 8," defending the reading of the Received Text in each of these passages. The writer is so inaccurate as to represent, at the very beginning of his essay, the words "in earth," in 1 John v. 8, as undisputed; though they are omitted in all the known Greek manuscripts written before the invention of printing, and are rejected as spurious by all the scholars who reject the rest of the passage in question. His account of the various readings of Acts xx. 28, and of the evidence for them, is also grossly inaccurate. Indeed, the article is full of misstatements, and appears to have been written by some one wholly ignorant of the literature of the last thirty years. The arguments adduced in favor of the genuineness of 1 John v. 7 are founded on the incorrect assertions and utterly exploded hypotheses of such writers as Nolan and Hales. The absence of the passage from all existing Greek manuscripts of any authority and from the ancient versions is explained by a reference to the order given to Eusebius by the Emperor Constantine, to have fifty copies of the Scriptures carefully transcribed for the use of the new churches in Constantinople.† Eusebius is supposed, on account of his "Arian proclivities," and "for a sinister purpose," to have omitted 1 John v. 7 from these copies. To complete the solution of the problem, we have only further to suppose that, though this remarkable text was before contained in all the Greek copies of

* Journal of Sacred Literature, April, 1858, pp. 171, 172.

† See Eusebius's Life of Constantine, IV. 36.

the Epistle possessed by Christians in Asia Minor, Syria, Palestine, Egypt, Greece, Italy, Gaul, and other parts of the world, to say nothing of the early versions, it was eliminated from all the manuscripts in the hands of the orthodox as well as of the Arians, *without discovery*, in an age of heated controversy on the subject of the Trinity. The corrupted copies were palmed off upon Athanasius and his followers, and the ancient versions made in the second and third centuries in Syria and Egypt were mutilated to correspond to them, so that no trace of the passage has been found in any manuscript copy of those versions, or in any Greek manuscript written before the invention of printing, or in the writings of any Greek father before the middle of the fourteenth century. Nobody ever missed it; and the fraud of Eusebius was first detected, some fifteen hundred years after its perpetration, by the sagacity of the Rev. Frederick Nolan!

After this satisfactory removal of the difficulty about the Greek manuscripts and the ancient versions, the reviewer complacently remarks, "If such is the light that Bishop Bloomfield is waiting for, we hope that his next edition may have it"; confounding, with the carelessness which characterizes the whole article, the Rev. S. T. Bloomfield, the editor of the Greek Testament, with Blomfield, the Bishop of London, and ignorant that Bloomfield, to whom he refers as "decidedly in favor of the passage," had twenty-five years ago abandoned the defence of it as hopeless. Bishop Blomfield had also long before expressed his belief of its spuriousness.*

In justice to the editors of the Boston Review, though they say that "evidently the time has not come to close the case," it should be stated that they supplement the article by giving quotations from Alford and Tregelles, which present the facts as they are.

The existence of such defences of the disputed passage as we have had occasion to notice must not mislead us as to the real state of the case. In the judgment of all scholars whose opinion is worthy of respect, the question, I believe, has long been regarded as settled. This statement, however, it may be well to

* See W. D. Conybeare's Theological Lectures, 2d edit., p 209.

confirm by definite references, and by quotations from the writings of the most eminent critics.

The text of the Three Heavenly Witnesses has been rejected as spurious in all the editions of the Greek Testament published within the present century which have any critical reputation among scholars; for example, in those of Knapp (1797, 5th edit. 1840), Matthæi (1804), Griesbach (smaller edit. 1805, larger 1806), Schott (1805, 4th edit. 1839), Tittmann (stereotype edit. 1820), Vater (1824), Lachmann (1831, larger edit. 1850), Bloomfield (in his 3d edit. 1839, and later editions),* Hahn (1840, new edit. 1861), Tischendorf (1841, 7th edit. 1859), Theile (1844, 8th stereotype edit. 1865), Wordsworth (1860),† Alford (1861, 2d edit. 1862), T. S. Green, Twofold New Testament (1865), and in the editions by the Catholics Gratz (1821, new edit. 1828) and Scholz (1836), whom I have already had occasion to mention.

* Bloomfield says in his Recensio Synoptica, Vol. VIII. p. 776 (London, 1828), "To me it appears *probable* that the verses are genuine"; in his *first* edition of the Greek Testament (1831), he regarded "the authenticity of the verses as, though doubtful, yet verging to probability"; in his *second* edition (1836), reprinted and stereotyped in this country in 1837, he thinks "we are neither authorized to receive the passage as indubitably genuine, nor, on the other hand, to reject it as indubitably spurious, but to wait for further evidence"; in his *third* edition (1839) he marks the words as spurious, and rejects them decidedly in his notes; in the *ninth* edition (1855) he expresses his conclusion as follows: "In short, the words cannot, with any due regard to those canons of criticism acted upon in all other cases throughout the writings of the New Testament, be regarded otherwise than as spurious. I find not a vestige of them in any one of the numerous Lamb. and Mus. manuscripts which I have collated."

The Rev. Edward Burton, D. D., Regius Professor of Divinity in the University at Oxford, in his edition of the Greek Testament (1831, 3d edit. 1848), brackets the passage, and remarks in a note, "There is great reason to think that all the words from ἐν τῷ οὐρανῷ [in heaven] to ἐν τῇ γῇ [on earth] are an interpolation." In his Bampton Lectures, p. 523, he rejects them, though with confessed reluctance, as spurious.

† Though Wordsworth rejects the disputed text as a gloss, he finds the doctrine of the Trinity, as Augustine and others had done before him, in the eighth verse, understanding by "the water" the Father, and by "the blood" the Son!

There is nearly the same agreement among all the translators and commentators of the present century, who have any reputation for learning and judgment. Accordingly the disputed passage is treated as spurious by Stolz (4th edit. 1804), Augusti (1805), Seiler (1806), Rosenmüller (5th edit. 1808), our countryman Charles Thomson in his translation of the Bible (1808), Hewlett (1812, also 1816), Adam Clarke (1817), Jaspis (2d edit. 1821), Boothroyd (1824, new edit. 1843), Lücke (1825, 2d edit. 1836), Rickli (1828), H. A. W. Meyer (1829), Paulus (1829), Grashof (1830), Granville Penn (1836, '37), De Wette (1837, 5th edit. by Brückner, 1863), Jachmann (1838), Baumgarten-Crusius (1845), Barnes (1847), Dr. Edward Ash (1849), Neander (1851, Eng. trans. 1852), Huther (1855, 2d edit. 1861), Düsterdieck (1856), Bunsen, *Bibelwerk*, Abth. I. Theil I. pp. clxxxvii.-cxciii. (1858), Ebrard (1859), Ewald (1861), Holtzmann, in Bunsen's *Bibelwerk* (1864), and the American Bible Union in its revised translation of the New Testament (1864).

The only recent commentators whom I have seen referred to as maintaining the genuineness of the passage in debate are J. E. F. Sander (1851), W. F. Besser (1851), and G. K. Mayer (1851), — all German writers. Sander speaks of the passage doubtfully, and enters into no full discussion of the question, merely opposing Griesbach's view of the testimony of Cyprian and one or two other Latin fathers. Besser and Mayer I have not examined; the latter is a Catholic. Sander and Besser are Lutheran clergymen, who have published a good many small popular and controversial works; but I am not aware that either of them has any reputation for critical scholarship.

Of the commentators whom I have named on the writings of John, the most universally esteemed, perhaps, is Lücke, Professor of Theology in the University of Bonn, and afterwards in that of Göttingen. In reference to 1 John v. 7, he observes: — "No result of modern criticism is more certain than that this passage is spurious." *

Most of the *popular* commentaries current in this country and

* Comm. über die Briefe des Ev. Johannes, 2[e] Aufl., pp. 294, 295; or p. 267, Eng. translation.

England either belong to the last century, or are the production of writers, like Thomas Scott, who have no pretension to critical learning.

The principal writers in defence of the doctrine of the Trinity in the present century, as Wardlaw, Stuart, and Dr. John Pye Smith, likewise agree in its rejection. Thus Professor Stuart says, "The text in 1 John v. 7 is beyond all question indefensible." * Dr. John Pye Smith, whose "Scripture Testimony to the Messiah" is perhaps the most learned and elaborate treatise in the English language on the deity of Christ, observes: "That some learned writers have of late professed themselves satisfied of the authenticity of this passage, while they advance nothing but surmises and conjectures, and mistakes almost incredible in the statement of facts, to counterbalance the weight of evidence on the other side, excites my astonishment and concern. . . . . The attempt to set aside the decision of impartial and honest criticism is painfully discreditable." †

Instead of giving, as it would be easy to do, a long list of the names of eminent Trinitarian scholars and divines of the present century, who have expressed incidentally their conviction of the spuriousness of this famous proof-text, I shall confine myself, in what follows, to those who have specially devoted themselves to the textual criticism of the New Testament in general, or who have elaborately discussed this subject in particular, since the publication of Mr. Orme's Memoir.

Dr. Samuel Lee, Regius Professor of Hebrew in the University of Cambridge, in his Prolegomena to Bagster's Polyglott Bible, also prefixed to his Novum Testamentum Syriacum, London, [1831,] 4to, discusses the genuineness of our "greatly vexed passage," and repudiates it as spurious. (Prol. vi. § 2, pp. 71 – 74.)

The Rev. Thomas Hartwell Horne, in his Introduction to the Holy Scriptures, has given a very full account of the evidence and

* Letters to Channing, new edition, in his "Miscellanies," Andover, 1846, p. 137.

† Scripture Testimony to the Messiah, third edition, Lond. 1837, Vol. III. pp. 127, 128; fifth edition (1859), Vol. II. pp. 253, 254. See also Wardlaw's Discourses on the Socinian Controversy, pp. 15, 16, Amer. edit.

arguments on both sides of the question respecting the controverted text. In the *fourth* edition of that work (London, 1824), reprinted at Philadelphia in 1825 in four volumes, octavo, he favored the genuineness of the passage, being misled by the inaccurate statements of Nolan, Hales, and Bishop Burgess. But the errors of these writers having been fully exposed by Oxlee, Turton, and others, he had the candor and honesty, in later editions, among them the eighth (1839), reprinted at Philadelphia in 1840, to abandon the passage as spurious. In the tenth edition of this work (1856), Vol. IV. pp. 355 – 384, Dr. Tregelles has made some valuable additions to Horne's account of the controversy. The literature of the subject is given in a bibliographical Appendix, pp. 384 – 388.

The Rev. J. Scott Porter, Professor of Sacred Criticism and Theology to the Association of Non-subscribing Presbyterians in Ireland, has given a good account of the facts of the case in his Principles of Textual Criticism (London, 1848), pp. 494 – 512. It is hardly necessary to say that he regards the disputed text as a manifest interpolation. Professor Porter, however, is a Unitarian. I mention this work particularly on account of the interesting information which it gives respecting the readings of the passage in certain ancient Latin manuscripts in the British Museum.

Dr. Samuel Davidson, in his Treatise on Biblical Criticism (1852), Vol. II. pp. 403 – 426, after a full discussion of the evidence on the subject, comes to the conclusion that the passage is "certainly spurious."

No English scholar of the present century has made so important contributions to the textual criticism of the New Testament, or has done so much to awaken a new interest in the subject, as Dr. Samuel Prideaux Tregelles. He has devoted himself with unwearied zeal and diligence for more than twenty-five years to the collation of manuscripts and the collection of materials for a new edition of the Greek Testament, of which the first part only, containing the Gospels, has yet been published. His treatise on the Textual Criticism of the New Testament, contained in Vol. IV. of Horne's Introduction, tenth edition, and also published separately, is an original work of the highest authority and value. Bleek, in his Introduction to the New Testament (Berlin, 1862), p. 34, strongly expresses the wish that it might be translated into German.* What, then, does Dr. Tregelles say of our passage?

"To enter into a formal discussion of the genuineness of the testimony of the Heavenly Witnesses, 1 John v. 7," he observes, "is really superfluous; for it would only be doing over again what has been done so repeatedly that there cannot be two opinions in the minds of those who now *know* the evidence, and are capable of appreciating its force. . . . . I only add, that *if* the words be considered genuine, then any addition of any kind, found in any manuscript (however recent), and supported by the later copies of any one version, in opposition to the more ancient, possesses as good a claim to be received and used as a portion of Holy Scripture." †

The most distinguished of the recent critical editors of the Greek Testament is Constantine Tischendorf, Professor of Theology in the University of Leipsic. Speaking of the text of the Three Heavenly Witnesses, he says: —

"That this spurious addition should continue to be published as a part of the Epistle, I regard as an impiety as well as an act of ignorance or rather of fraud. The relation of the passage to criticism is such, that we must exclude it without hesitation from the sacred volume, unless the entire art of criticism, with all its apparatus of ancient witnesses, is to be regarded as worthless and rejected. Such being the case, what temerity it is, what contempt of the truth delivered by the sacred writers, to insert those words into the text, through fear that by their removal the doctrine of the divine Trinity may be endangered!" ‡

* I may mention incidentally, that Bleek, whose "History of the Text of the New Testament," in the work referred to, may be regarded as the best recent German treatise on the subject, emphatically rejects 1 John v. 7 as spurious. — Einleit. in d. N. T., p. 593. So Reuss, *Geschichte der heiligen Schriften Neuen Testaments*, i. e. "History of the Sacred Writings of the New Testament," third edition (1860, fourth edition 1864), § 360.

† Account of the Printed Text of the Greek New Testament, London, 1854, 8vo, pp. 226, 227.

‡ Novum Testamentum Triglottum, 1854, Prolegom., p. cx.

One of the best books illustrating the application of critical principles to the text of the New Testament is the "Course of Developed Criticism on Passages of the New Testament materially affected by Various Readings," published at London in 1856 by the Rev. Thomas Sheldon Green, late Fellow of Christ's College, Cambridge, the author of a "Treatise on the Grammar of the New Testament," and, more recently, of a new translation of the Greek Testament accompanied by a critical edition of the original text, entitled "The Twofold New Testament," &c. In regard to 1 John v. 7, Mr. Green observes:—

"It is not too much to say that, if a critic could be supposed to be debarred from all documentary evidence on either side in the present case, except those few MSS. which exhibit the verse, and the only version that has it, namely, the common text of the Vulgate, the circumstances which even thus would come under his notice, would form a sufficient ground for its condemnation as a spurious accretion." *

In 1861 the Rev. Frederick Henry Scrivener, of Trinity College, Cambridge, Rector of St. Gerrans, Cornwall, published "A Plain Introduction to the Criticism of the New Testament," containing much valuable information, the result of the author's personal investigations. Mr. Scrivener has also earned the gratitude of biblical students by his published collations of manuscripts, and his very careful and scholarly editions of the *Codex Augiensis* and the *Codex Bezæ*. In speaking of the controversy on 1 John v. 7, after referring to Porson, he adds:—

"The *Letters* of that prince of scholars, and the contemporaneous researches of Herbert Marsh, have completely decided the contest: Bishop Burgess alone, while yet among us [d. 1837], clung obstinately to a few scattered outposts after the main field of battle had been lost beyond recovery.

"On the whole, therefore, we need not hesitate to declare our conviction that the disputed words were not written by St. John: that they were originally brought into Latin copies in Africa from the margin, where they had been placed as a pious and orthodox gloss on v. 8: that from the Latin they crept into two or three

* Course of Developed Criticism, pp. 183, 184.

late Greek codices, and thence into the printed Greek text, a place to which they had no rightful claim." *

The best critical edition of the Greek Testament with English notes is, I believe, universally admitted to be that of the Rev. Henry Alford, D. D., Dean of Canterbury, the first volume of which was published in 1849, and has already passed through at least five editions. The volume containing the Epistles of John (Vol. IV. Part II. of the work) first appeared in 1861; 2d edit., 1862. The following extract from his note on the passage is sufficiently explicit: —

"The question of the genuineness of the words read in the Received Text at the end of verse 7, has been discussed, as far as external grounds are concerned, in the digest; and it has been seen, that unless pure caprice is to be followed in the criticism of the sacred text, *there is not the shadow of a reason for supposing them genuine.* Even the supposed citations of them in early Latin Fathers have now, on closer examination, disappeared. Something remains to be said on internal grounds, on which we have full right to enter, now that the other is secured. And on these grounds it must appear, on any fair and unprejudiced consideration, that the words are 1) alien from the context: 2) in themselves incoherent, and betraying another hand than the Apostle's." This Alford proceeds to show.

Since the date of Mr. Orme's Memoir (1830) many Greek manuscripts containing the First Epistle of John have been brought to light, or collated for the first time, by Scholz, Tischendorf, Scrivener, and others. It may be well, therefore, to give here a brief summary of the present state of the evidence for and against the genuineness of the disputed text. For details, one may consult the recent critical editions of Tischendorf and Alford.

The number of Greek manuscripts, including lectionaries, which are known to omit the text of the Heavenly Witnesses, is more than *two hundred and twenty-five*, and probably not less than *two hundred and fifty*.† Among these are the Sinaitic and the

* Plain Introd. to the Criticism of the New Test., pp. 462, 463.

† See the Rev. A. W. Grafton's statement in Alford's Greek Test., Vol. IV. pp. 269, 270, 2d edit.; Scrivener's Plain Introduction, p. 459.

Vatican, of the fourth century, and the Alexandrine, of the fifth. The disputed words, on the other hand, are found in the text of but *two* Greek manuscripts, one (No. 162) of the fifteenth or sixteenth century, the other (34) of the sixteenth, and neither of any critical importance. (See before, pp. 181, 195.) The variations in the readings of these two manuscripts, the omission of the article, and their conformity to the Latin Vulgate in other places, make it in the highest degree probable that they derived the passage by translation from that version. The disputed text is also found in the *margin* of two other Greek manuscripts (Nos. 69 and 173) in writing not earlier than the sixteenth century. In this account I have not noticed the *Codex Ravianus* at Berlin, which has been proved to be a forgery; or a Wolfenbüttel manuscript of the seventeenth century, the *Codex Guelpherbytanus* D, already referred to (see p. 194), both of which, as not possessing the slightest authority, are excluded by the critical editors from their lists.

The disputed words are also wanting in all the ancient versions namely, in the Peshito Syriac (Cent. ii.), the Thebaic or Sahidic (ii. or iii.), the Memphitic or Coptic (iii. or iv.), the Æthiopic iv. or v.), the Armenian (v.), the Harclean or Philoxenian Syriac (made A. D. 508, revised 616), the several Arabic versions, and the Slavonic (ix.), though it has been foisted into some *editions* of the Peshito, the Armenian, and the Slavonic, in opposition to the authority of the manuscripts.* Nor do they properly belong either to the Old Latin (Cent. ii.), or to the Vulgate (Cent. iv.), though these versions have been claimed by the advocates of the passage. The Old Latin has already been spoken of, in the remarks on Wiseman's theory (see before, p. 188). That the pas-

* The history of its introduction into several printed editions of the Syriac is instructive. Tremellius, in his edition of the Peshito published in 1569, left a blank space for it in the text, and placed *his own translation of it into Syriac* in a note; Gutbier (1664) inserted this translation in his text, and in his Notes (1667) remarks: — "Since it is well known that the Arians have in this place neither spared the Greek text itself, nor the Oriental versions, we have inserted this verse, which is wanting in other editions, from the Notes of Tremellius." After him, Schaaf inserted it in his edition (1709 and 1717).

sage is also an interpolation in the Latin Vulgate is proved by the fact, that, though contained in a large majority of the manuscripts of that version, it is wanting in the two oldest and best, the *Codex Amiatinus* written about A. D. 541, and the *Codex Fuldensis* of about the same age, and in more than *fifty* others, many of them of high antiquity; by its various readings and uncertain position in the manuscripts which do contain it, in many of the older ones it being found only in the margin, or after the eighth verse; and finally, by the total want of reference to it in the writings of very many of the older Latin fathers who had occasion to cite it, including Jerome, the author of the version. The first Latin writer who has clearly quoted it is Vigilius Tapsensis, who flourished near the end of the fifth century; it is quoted by a few other Latin writers previous to the ninth century, and by many after that date. The oldest manuscript of the Vulgate which contains it belongs probably to the seventh or eighth century.*

This unanimous testimony of ALL THE KNOWN GREEK MANUSCRIPTS WRITTEN BEFORE THE INVENTION OF PRINTING, and of ALL THE ANCIENT VERSIONS, is strikingly confirmed by the absence of the passage from the Scripture quotations of ALL THE GREEK FATHERS BEFORE THE FOURTEENTH CENTURY, though several of them, as Gregory Nazianzen and Cyril of Alexandria, with great ingenuity extract proofs of the Trinity from the verses before and after it.

SUCH being the state of the case, what must we think of those who in this nineteenth century quote the passage as a proof-text in sermons preached to the unlearned, or publish it in books designed for popular circulation, for Sunday Schools and Bible Classes, without a hint of its spuriousness? What must we think of those, who, noticing the fact that its genuineness has been disputed, denounce their fellow-Christians as arbitrarily and

* I refer to the La Cava manuscript; see before, p. 189. It is remarkable, that both this manuscript, and the other oldest Latin manuscript which contains 1 John v. 7, — the *Speculum* published by Mai, — support also the spurious Epistle of Paul to the Laodiceans. So No. 11,852 (9th cent.) of the *Additional MSS.* in the British Museum. See Westcott's art. on the Vulgate in Smith's Dictionary of the Bible, III. 1713, note q.

wickedly rejecting it from repugnance to the doctrine it is supposed to teach? What must we think of the managers of religious Societies, who publish editions of the New Testament for family use, "with notes designed *to give the results of critical investigation*," * in which there is *no* note on a passage like this? We may not assume to pass judgment on the character of the *persons* concerned, for our knowledge of their motives and circumstances is necessarily imperfect; but there would seem to be room for but one opinion among honest and intelligent men, when their attention is directed to the subject, in respect to the practices themselves.

Again; how long shall this notorious interpolation be circulated in the popular versions of the Bible without mark of doubt, and be imposed upon the unlearned as a part of what they are taught to revere as "the word of God"? In regard to Luther's German version, in which it is well known to have been inserted long after his death in defiance of his expressed wishes, it would seem that there could be no hesitation in striking it from the text. The question in regard to the common English version presents greater difficulty. But I will quote, for the benefit of those interested, two expressions of opinion on the matter.

"Fear of the Church of Rome on the one hand," says a recent writer in the Edinburgh Review, "and of the Socinians on the other, appears to have induced the half-hearted authorities of the Church of England to retain this known interpolation in a version which was to be the sole appeal of the unlearned vulgar. And we cannot consider it creditable to our Church, that this spurious passage is annually read to the laity in the Epistle for the First Sunday after Easter, and in one of the lessons on Trinity Sunday." †

The following is from an article on "The Ethics of Editorship," by a writer whose name will command universal respect: —

"It is difficult to decide how far a received text ought to be altered upon the discovery of its incorrectness. And with regard

* These words are from the title-page of an edition of the New Testament recently published by the American Tract Society, New York.

† Edinburgh Review for July, 1865; CXXII. 113.

to the text of the Scriptures this question becomes one of great delicacy and importance. . . . . But what shall we say of a passage like 1 John v. 7, in which all competent judges concede that there is an interpolation, and which many persons omit when they read the context in public. Do not truth and honesty require that such a passage should be struck out of our English Bibles, a passage which Luther would not express in his translation, and which did not creep into the German Bible until nearly fifty years after his death? Would the shock of its insertion in brackets, or of its disappearance from our version, do as much harm as the display of Christian honesty and of true reverence to the genuine word of God would do good? We suggest that a number of biblical critics, of approved character for orthodoxy, should move in this matter, and demand at least a careful consideration of this text. We cannot but believe that the state of the case is so plain as to admit of but one conclusion. And we cannot think that anything would prevent the change from being effected, but an unworthy timidity, which is neither Christian nor upright." *

* The Rev. Theodore D. Woolsey, D.D., President of Yale College, in the New Englander for August, 1852; X. 384.

## Note to Page 185, Line 27.

It has since been shown, by the researches of Dr. Klose, that 1 John v. 7 was interpolated in Luther's version as early as 1582, in an edition published at Frankfort, in quarto. See the note on the passage in Huther's Commentary (in German), 2d edit., 1861, p. 211. *Tanzer* in Huther's note is a misprint for *Panzer*.

# INDEX.



N

www.ingramcontent.com/pod-product-compliance
Lightning Source LLC
LaVergne TN
LVHW050528100826
845148LV00002B/477

* 9 7 8 1 4 2 5 5 1 9 6 9 8 *